LANDSCAPE
WALES

Julie

on The Occasion of your wedding

in case you get home sick

love Ben + Esther
x x x
x

GRAFFEG

Published by Graffeg
Paperback first published
Spring 2004 size 250 x 200mm
Copyright © Graffeg 2004
ISBN 0-9544334-3-2

Also published by Graffeg in
hardback Autumn 2003
size 300 x 250mm
ISBN 0-9544334-1-6

Graffeg, Radnor Court,
256 Cowbridge Road East
Cardiff CF5 1GZ Wales UK
Tel +44(0) 2920 377312
sales@graffeg.com
www.graffeg.com

Graffeg are hereby identified
as the authors of this work in
accordance with section 77
of the Copyrights, Designs
and Patents Act 1988.

All images © Photographers

A CIP Catalogue record for
this book is available from
the British Library.

Designed and produced by
Peter Gill & Associates
sales@petergill.com
www.petergill.com

LANDSCAPE
WALES

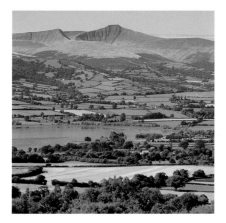

Llangorse Lake
Brecon Beacons
Photographer, Jeremy Moore.

Powerful images have been captured by photographers at The Photolibrary Wales taking you to many inspiring locations around Wales – from climbing the spectacular mountains of Snowdonia and surfing on the dramatic Pembrokeshire coast to the gentler attractions of the lowlands and idyllic river valleys.

Edited by Steve Benbow and Peter Gill, foreword by Bryn Terfel written by David Williams

Published by Graffeg.

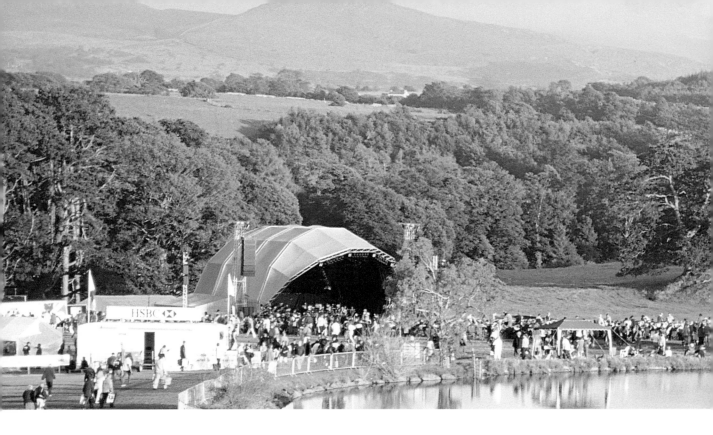

Bryn Terfel's Faenol Festival,
held each August, is the place
to hear stars of opera, musical
theatre and Welsh music
perform against the
incomparable backdrop
of Snowdonia.
Photographer, David Williams.

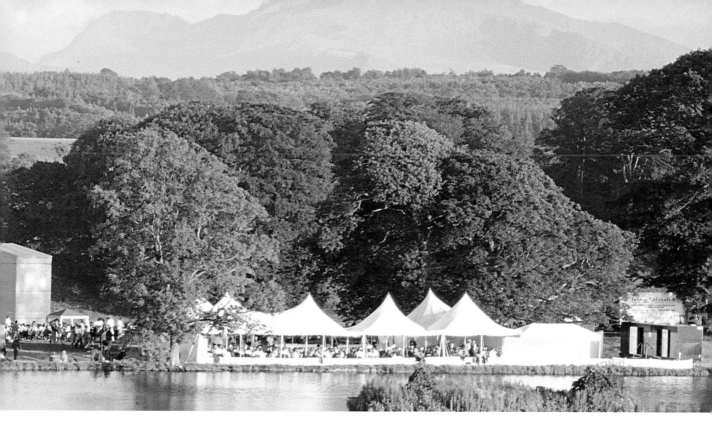

Foreword

I count myself fortunate to live among the wonderful people and scenery of Wales – in one of the most exquisitely varied and deeply fascinating landscapes in the world. From Anglesey to the Severn estuary, from Pembrokeshire to the Clwydian Hills, this really is one of the most agreeable places imaginable in which to live, work and enjoy the great outdoors.

Wales is an ancient land, both in geological features and in its long history of human endeavour. Over the centuries, the communities that made their lives here founded the rich cultural traditions – in music, poetry, literature and art – that mean so much to me.

The Faenol estate near Bangor, site of my annual music festival, was built on fortunes made from slate quarrying. Now used for cultural and business events, it is fitting that it also enjoys a new lease of life as a centre teaching stonemasonry and other skills used in conserving historic buildings.

The international performers who accept my invitation to sing at the Faenol Festival are always delighted by the wonders they see, and by the welcome they receive, here in Wales.

I invite you to visit my wondrous homeland and – hopefully inspired by the remarkable pictures in this book – to seek out your own favourite places to visit again and again, or to look back upon in your mind's eye from far away.

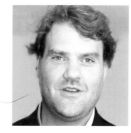

Bryn Terfel CBE

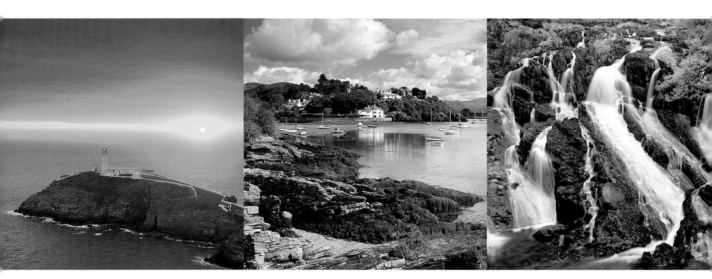

Introduction

Visitors to Wales have long appreciated the wealth of attractive and accessible landscape to be found within the compact dimensions of this fascinating part of the United Kingdom. Imposing mountains, sheltered valleys, a dramatic coastline, glittering lakes, chuckling streams, silent forests and tidy fields give shape and character – in endlessly pleasing variety – to this enormously appealing country.

The ever-changing seasons enrich the mix, each adding its own character to the scene. The freshness of woodland in spring, the haze-softened lushness of summer meadows and the 'mists and mellow fruitfulness' of autumn contrast with the clarity of distant mountains on a frosty morning, or the mesmerising power of a winter storm pounding a rocky coast.

In this book, we highlight the splendours of this remarkable land. Our national parks – Snowdonia, the Brecon Beacons and the Pembrokeshire Coast – contain features and environments of international importance. Elsewhere, the landscape includes farmland, undisturbed natural habitat and places where people enjoy a wide range of leisure activities, from the most relaxing to the daringly energetic.

The land, as we see it today, represents a two-way process. Firstly, its relative remoteness has, over many centuries, shaped the individuality of the people who live and work here, and enabled their vibrant culture to survive. Secondly, the hand of mankind has tamed much of the terrain through farming, forestry, quarrying, mining and other occupations on and beneath its surface.

Farming remains the most visible industry – around 80% of Wales owes its appearance to agriculture. Our farmers excel at delivering produce of the

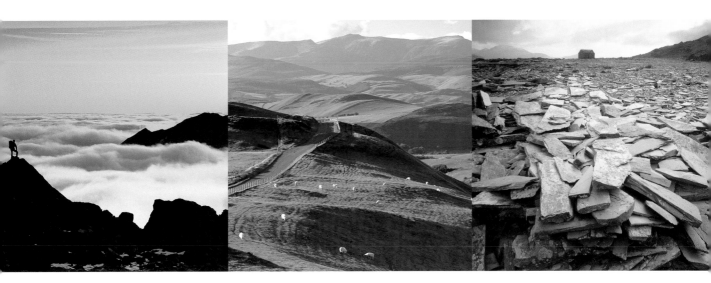

highest quality, which is now winning a world-wide profile, while recognising the importance of maintaining a balance with nature. Rural Wales is home to a diverse and advanced economy, while industrial communities enjoy a dramatic natural backdrop.

Tourism, one of Wales's major industries, celebrates the outstanding attractiveness of the landscape and encourages active enjoyment of the great outdoors. Our terrain provides the perfect challenge for the world's leading rally drivers.

Whether you seek adventurous pursuits or more gentle pleasures, Wales has many excellent places to stay and provides tremendous opportunities to participate in open-air activities and interests.

The quiet joys of a country walk, birdwatching or pony trekking – or the thrills of surfing, sailing or mountaineering – all give a very real sensation of being close to nature, while extending your knowledge and skills into new realms.

From spectacular, panoramic views to secret corners of immense charm, and from pristine nature reserves to the bustling countryside of farms, villages and towns, this small, but perfectly formed, corner of our planet impresses and delights in ways that raise the spirits.

If you enjoy spending time in landscapes that please the eye and refresh the soul – in captivating surroundings of spaciousness and tranquillity – then you need look no further than Wales.

David Williams

Contents

Anglesey

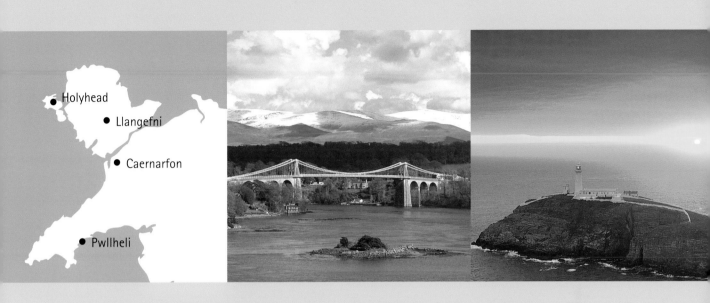

Separated from the rest of Wales by the Menai Strait and the mountains of Snowdonia, Anglesey enjoys a sensation of being removed from the cares of the world. Ancient historic sites, idyllic beaches and a patchwork of gently undulating farmland give the island an enchanting atmosphere all its own.

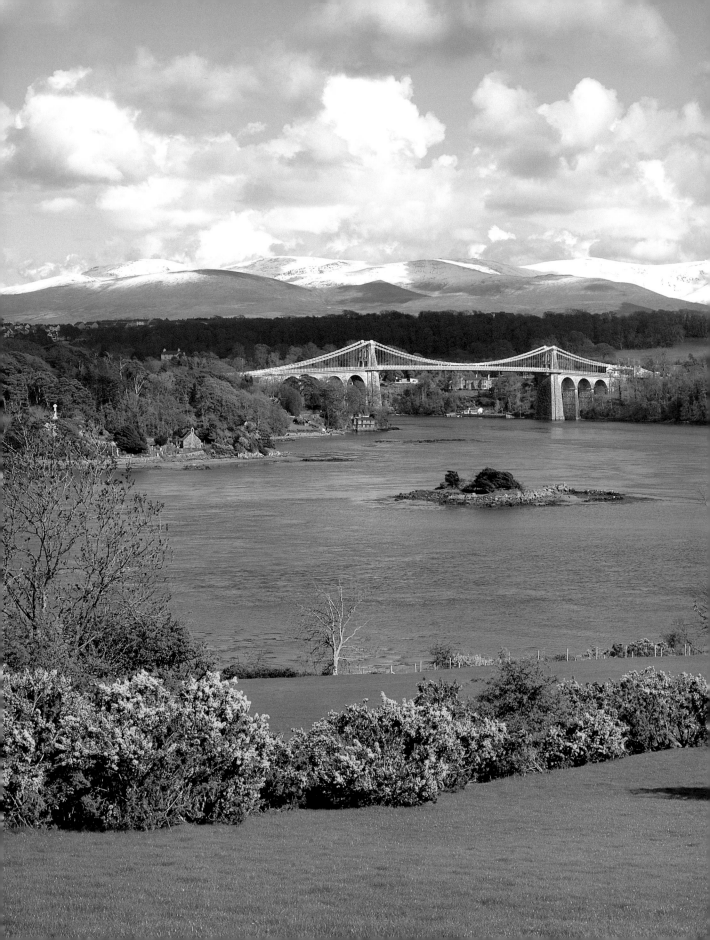

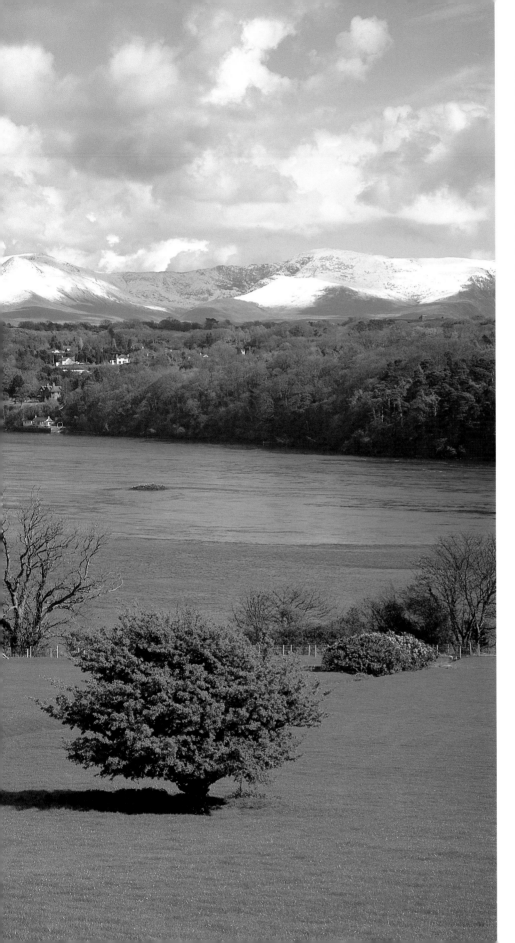

The Menai Strait
Separating Anglesey from Gwynedd, the Menai Strait is designated a Special Area of Conservation under European guidelines which recognise that the natural environment is one of Wales's greatest assets. View the Menai Strait from the A55 over Robert Stephenson's Britannia Bridge, or from Thomas Telford's graceful suspension bridge, which has footpaths either side. This view is from the A5, west of Menai Bridge. Photographer, Aled Hughes.

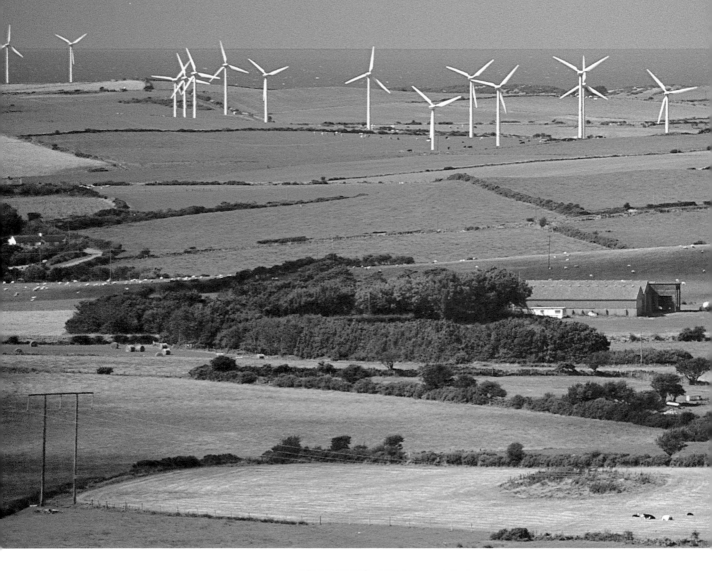

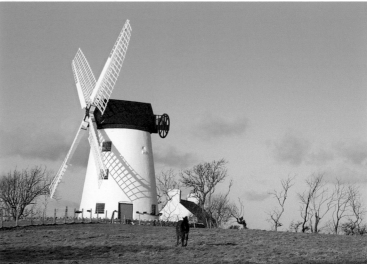

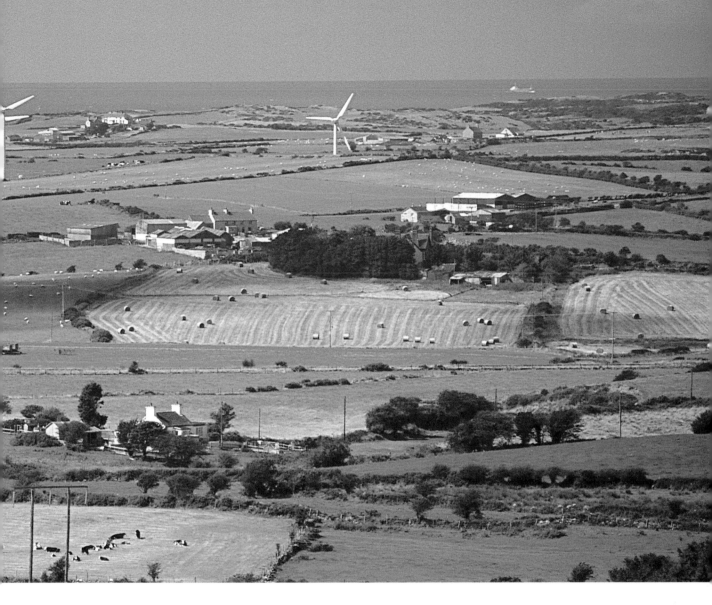

Llynnon Mill

Anglesey once grew more wheat, barley and oats than any other region of Wales and had around 100 mills, powered by wind or water. The millers who produced the essential flour were respected members of the community. Watch the miller at Llynnon, the only working windmill in Wales, grinding flour – and take a bag home to bake your own bread. Walk the three-mile Mills Trail to Melin Howell, a restored water mill – and reflect upon distant views of modern turbines at Llyn Alaw wind farm. Photographer, Derec Owen.

Granary of Wales

Rich soils have long sustained livestock and arable farming – 12th-century traveller Giraldus Cambrensis described Anglesey as 'The Granary of Wales'. Diversification into tourism, premium-quality foods, and even harvesting the wind, is an increasing trend. Visit Oriel Ynys Môn at Llangefni to learn how Anglesey's inhabitants have interacted with the land since prehistoric times. Photographer, Paul Kay.

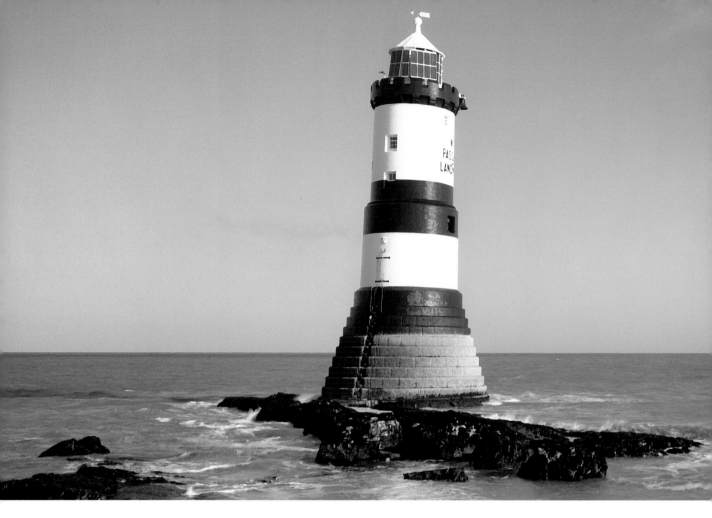

Penmon and Puffin Island
Black Point lighthouse marks the eastern tip of Anglesey and the entrance to the Menai Strait. Puffin Island takes its Welsh name, Ynys Seiriol, from the 6th-century saint who is buried there. Check on Beaumaris Pier for details of boat trips around Puffin Island.
Photographer, Aled Hughes.

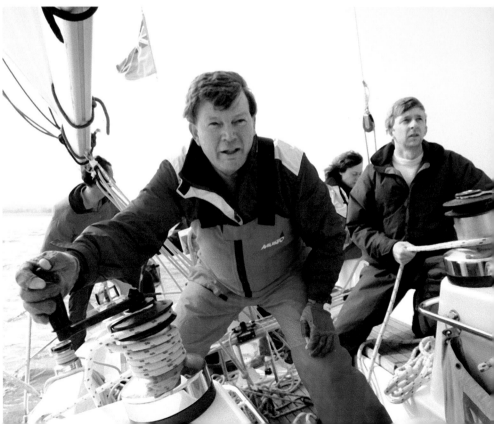

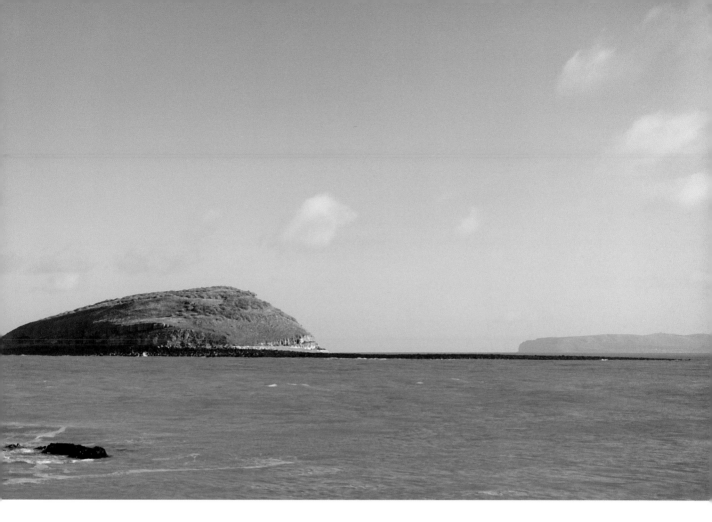

Yachting

For yacht and boat owners, Anglesey has it all – from Holyhead's busy harbour to remote and peaceful coves, from sheltered bays ideal for beginners to the navigational challenge of the Menai Strait. You could spend a lifetime exploring the coast of Anglesey, from the sailing centres of Holyhead and Beaumaris. Photographer, David Williams.

South Stack

The spectacular cliffs that plunge into the sea at South Stack, near Holyhead, are home to thousands of seabirds. The complex rock folds near the footbridge to the lighthouse are of pre-Cambrian origin – Wales gave its Latin name to the earliest era in the geology of our planet. Visit the RSPB visitor centre, Ellin's Tower, in early summer to view seabirds nesting on precarious ledges. Photographer, Steve Lewis.

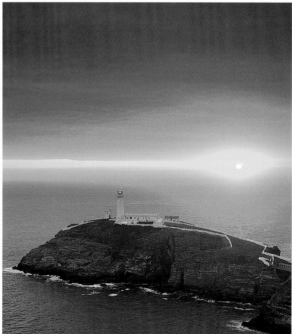

Northern Snowdonia

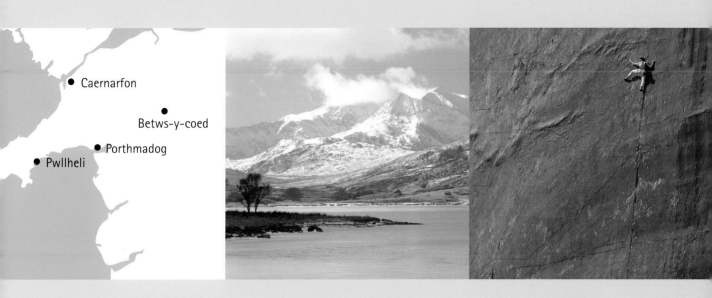

Snowdonia is the largest national park in Wales.
Its dramatic mountains and magnificent valleys,
carved by glaciers during the last Ice Age,
attract walkers, climbers, canoeists and cyclists –
and support patterns of upland farming that
have changed little in a thousand years.

• Caernarfon

• Betws-y-coed

• Porthmadog

• Pwllheli

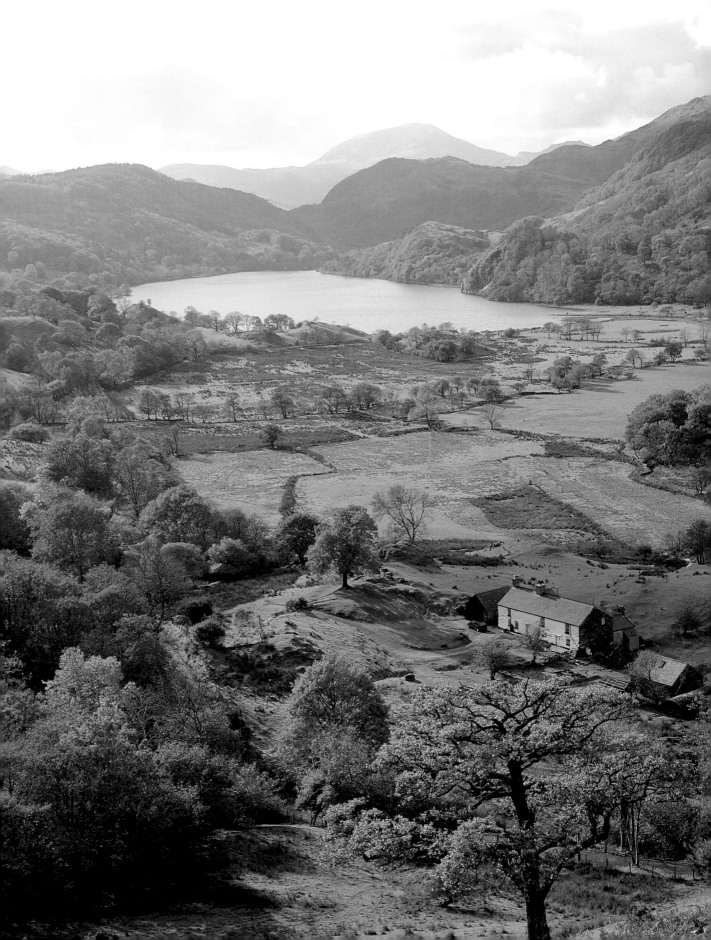

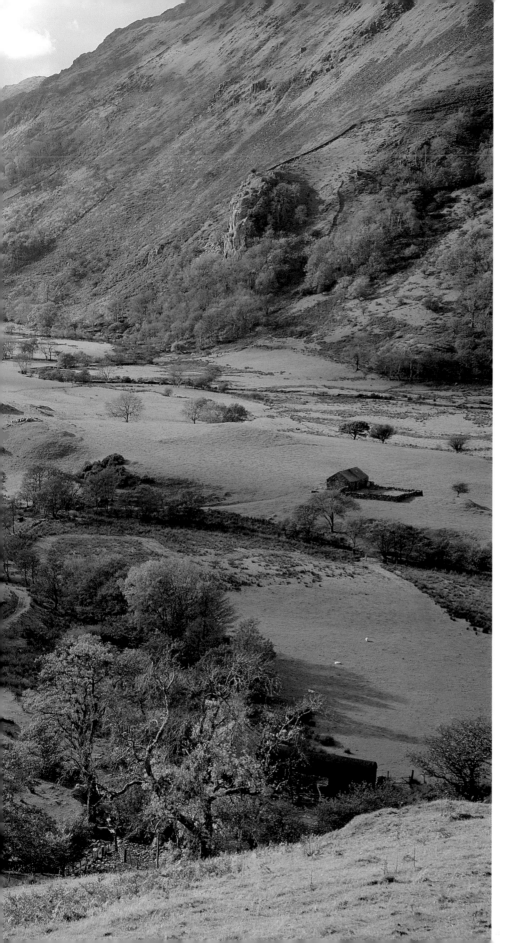

Nant Gwynant
At Dinas Emrys, a rock outcrop beyond the lake, the red dragon of Wales is said to have fought the white dragon of the Saxons, in the presence of Merlin the Magician, thus becoming the inspiration for the Welsh flag. Take the winding A458 from Beddgelert to a car park high above Nant Gwynant – for views, weather permitting, of Snowdon. Photographer, Chris Warren.

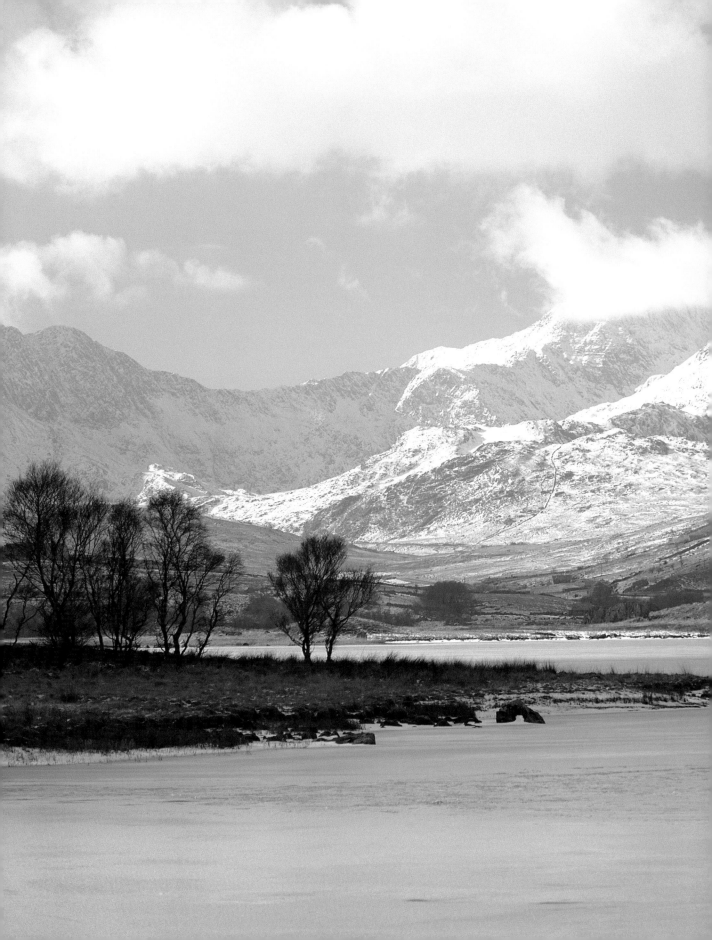

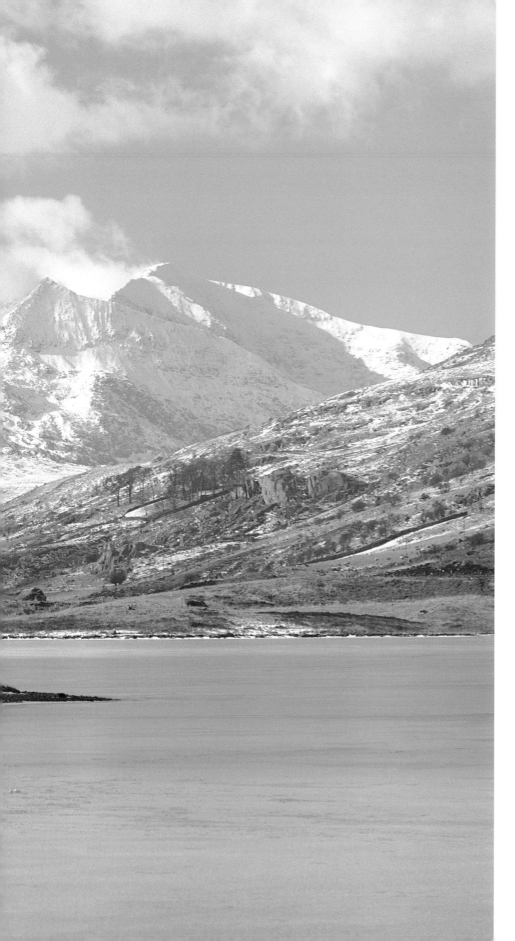

Snowdon

The classic view of Snowdon is from the direction of Capel Curig. The pyramidal peak of Snowdon itself – Yr Wyddfa – is serenely counter-balanced by the other summits of the group. Reaching the 3,560ft (1,085m) summit of Snowdon can be as easy or as difficult as you choose. Take the Snowdon Mountain Railway from Llanberis, or follow one of several paths – dress appropriately, know how to use map and compass, and stay within your limits. Photographer, Chris Warren.

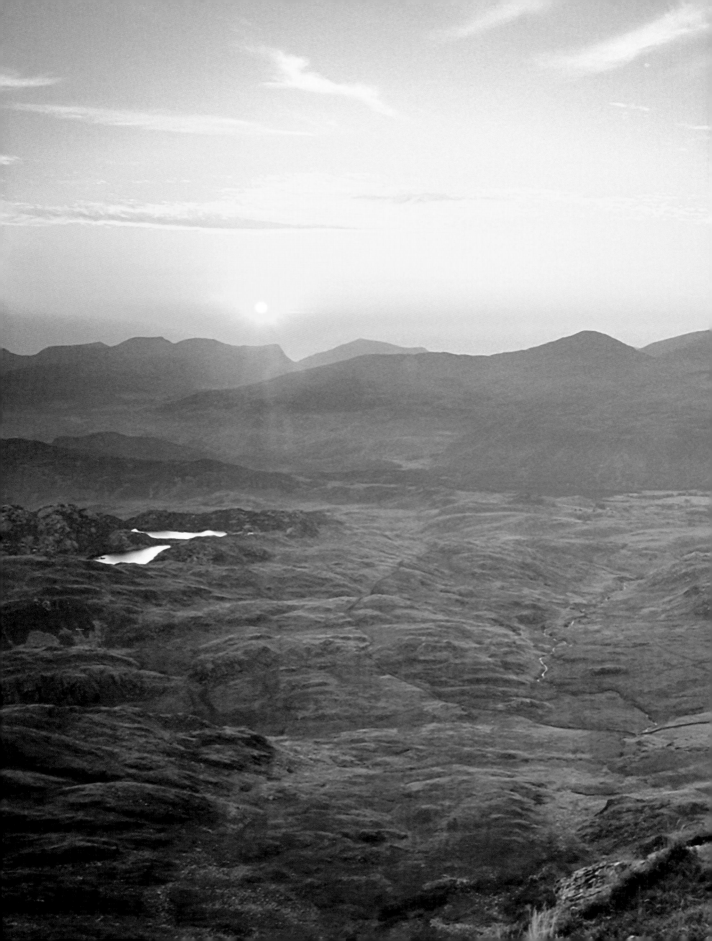

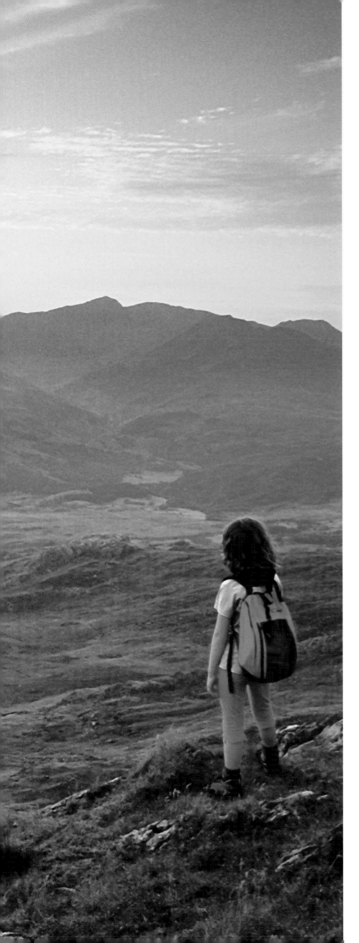

Nantlle Ridge and Snowdon from Cnicht

There are areas of Wales that seem empty, but which contain much evidence of human settlement. Prehistoric monuments, Iron Age forts, Roman roads, Medieval castles, ancient field boundaries and countless abandoned mines and quarries remind us of mankind's long presence in this land. The National Trust and CADW – Welsh Historic Monuments care for important landscapes and sites across the whole of Wales – their maps and publications will lead you to hidden treasures. Photographer, Dave Newbould.

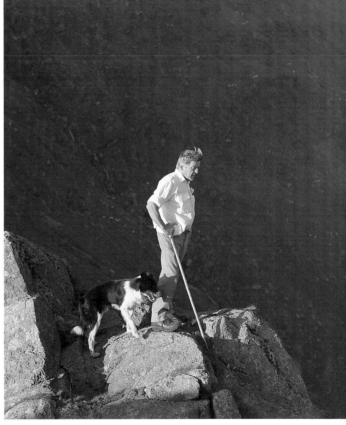

Sheep farmer

Sheep farmers communicate with their famously intelligent Border Collies through whistles and calls, as they follow the ancient rhythms of transhumance – moving sheep flocks up and down the mountain according to the season. Scan the hillsides, especially in spring or autumn, for sprinting sheepdogs responding to the commands of a shepherd as they corral ever-growing accumulations of reluctant sheep. Photographer, Steve Peake.

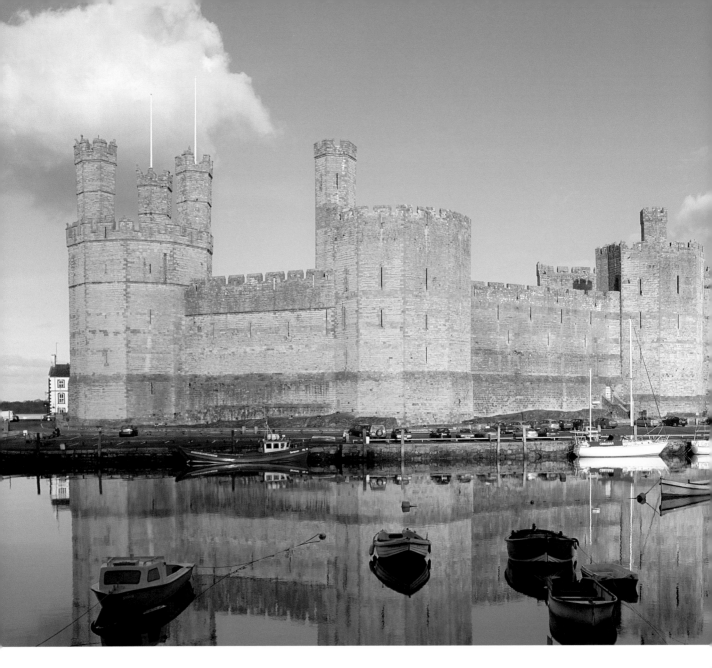

Tryfan

The Ogwen Valley, with Tryfan as its centrepiece and the mighty Carneddau to the north, gives a tremendous sense of space and remoteness – and yet there are working hill farms up here, where farmers and flocks brave whatever the weather throws at them. Park near Lake Ogwen and walk up to Cwm Idwal – taking in breathtaking views of Nant Ffrancon's wide valley – to see the textbook example of a glaciated landscape, as described by Charles Darwin.
Photographer, Jeremy Moore.

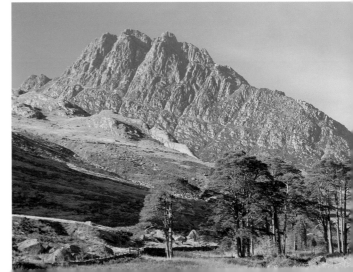

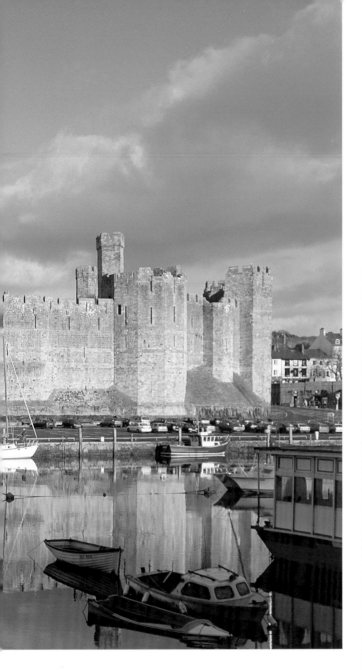

Caernarfon Castle

Caernarfon Castle is the largest of the fortresses built by Edward I to control the mountainous region of Gwynedd, following the defeat of Llywelyn ap Gruffudd, the last Welsh prince, in 1282. Today, the town is one of the most vigorously Welsh in its everyday life and language.

Climb the battlements to understand the scale of this intimidating structure – and to enjoy magnificent views of northern Snowdonia. Photographer, David Angel.

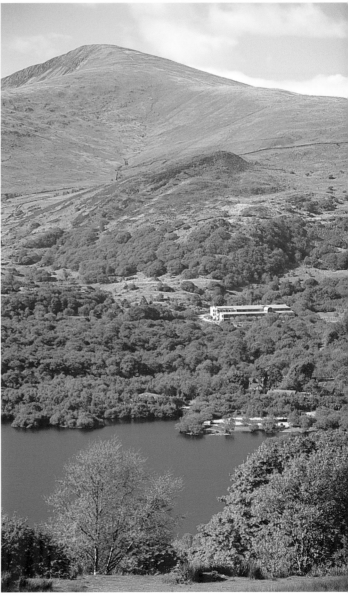

Glyn Rhonwy, Llanberis

Not everyone in Snowdonia works in tourism or agriculture – other industries have located in and around the national park, such as this manufacturer of medical diagnostic equipment in the shadow of Snowdon. The story of the slate industry is told at the Welsh Slate Museum in Llanberis, a National Museums and Galleries of Wales site.

Tour the Electric Mountain exhibition and Dinorwig hydro-electric power station deep inside the mountain nearby.
Photographer, Ray Wood.

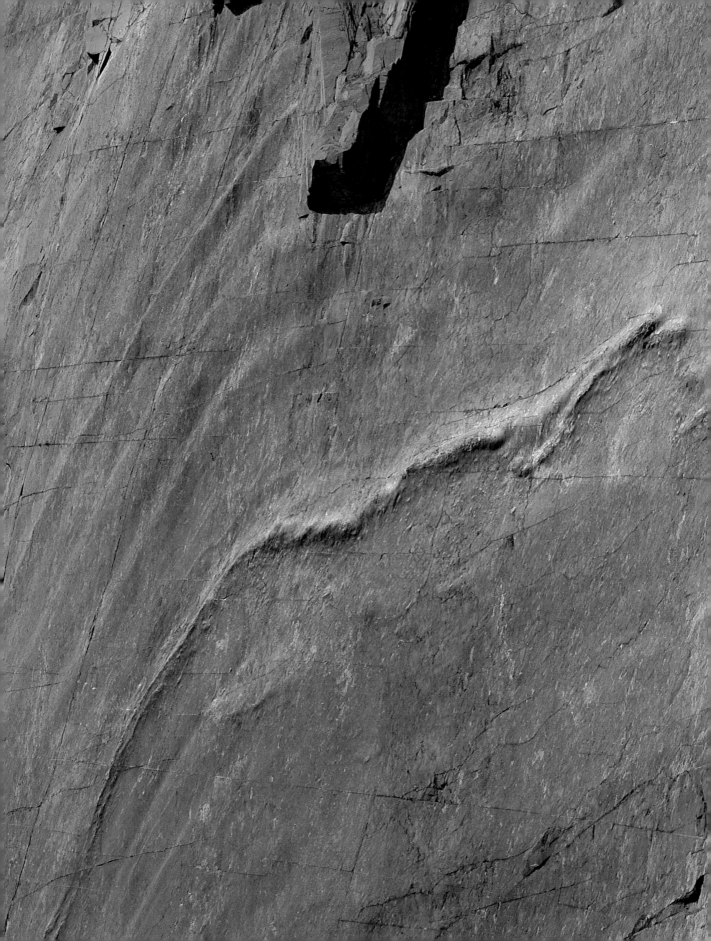

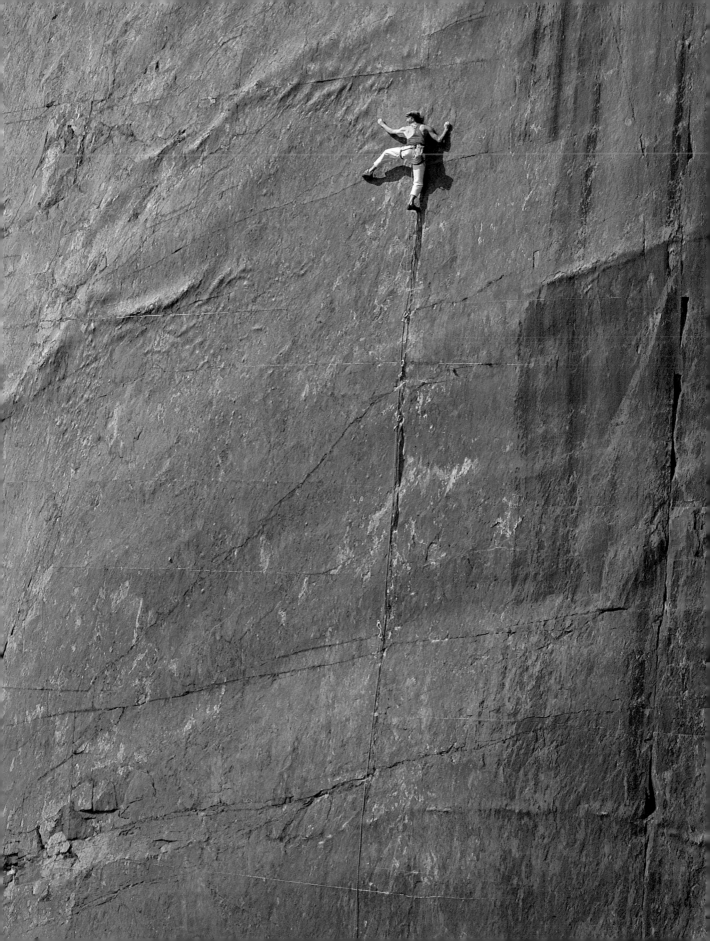

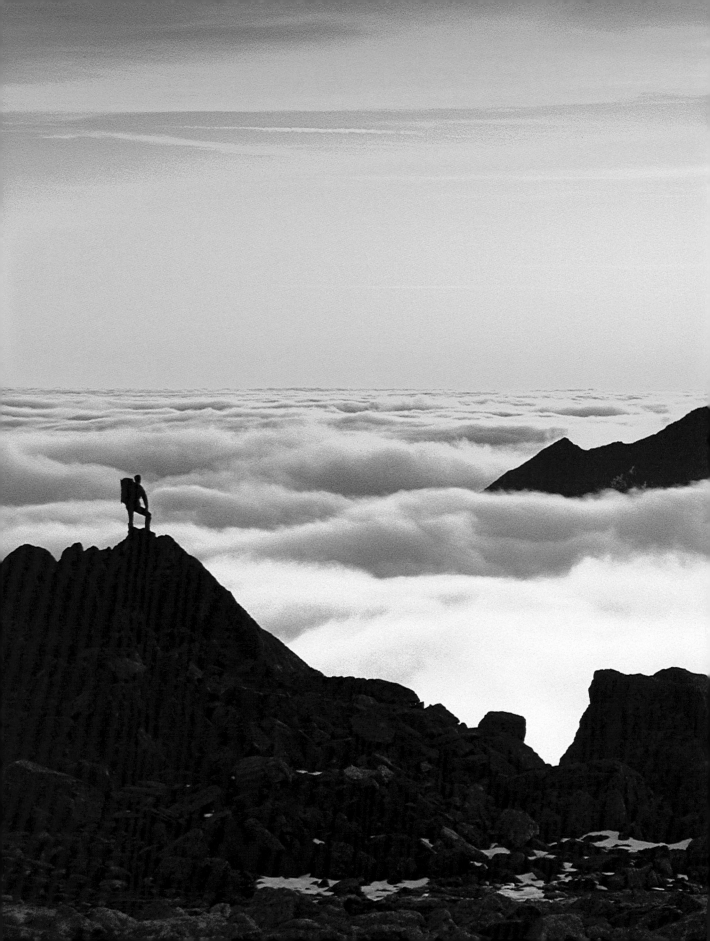

Llanberis Pass Pages 26/27
Snowdonia's mountaineering
credentials are impeccable –
the climbers who conquered
Everest in 1953 trained here.
Today's rock athletes seek
seemingly impossible routes
that demand great strength
and technical ability. The
region's top climbing locations
include Dinas Cromlech,
Clogwyn Du'r Arddu and the
Idwal Slabs. The National
Mountaineering Centre,
Plas-y-Brenin, provides
courses to suit all abilities.
Photographer, Ray Wood.

Lliwedd from Crib Goch
William Wordsworth, in the
conclusion to 'The Prelude',
describes climbing Snowdon
overnight from Beddgelert
to watch the sunrise, and
emerging above 'a huge
sea of mist' – a treat that
occasionally rewards
walkers on the high ridges.
The strenuous circuit of the
Snowdon Horseshoe, from
Pen y Pass, is the ultimate
mountain walk. It demands
a high level of fitness and
experience, and a cool head
for negotiating the knife-edge
ridges of Crib Goch.
Photographer, Dave Newbould.

Llŷn Peninsula

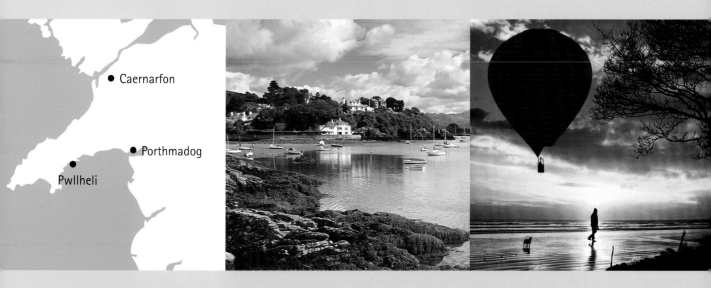

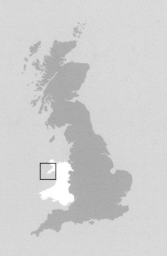

From the Stone Age axe factory on Mynydd Rhiw to the Celtic hill fort at Tre'r Ceiri, from sacred Bardsey Island to battle-worn Criccieth Castle, there are places in Llŷn that convey a tangible sense of history. It's a popular holiday area too, with harbours, beaches, golf courses and family attractions.

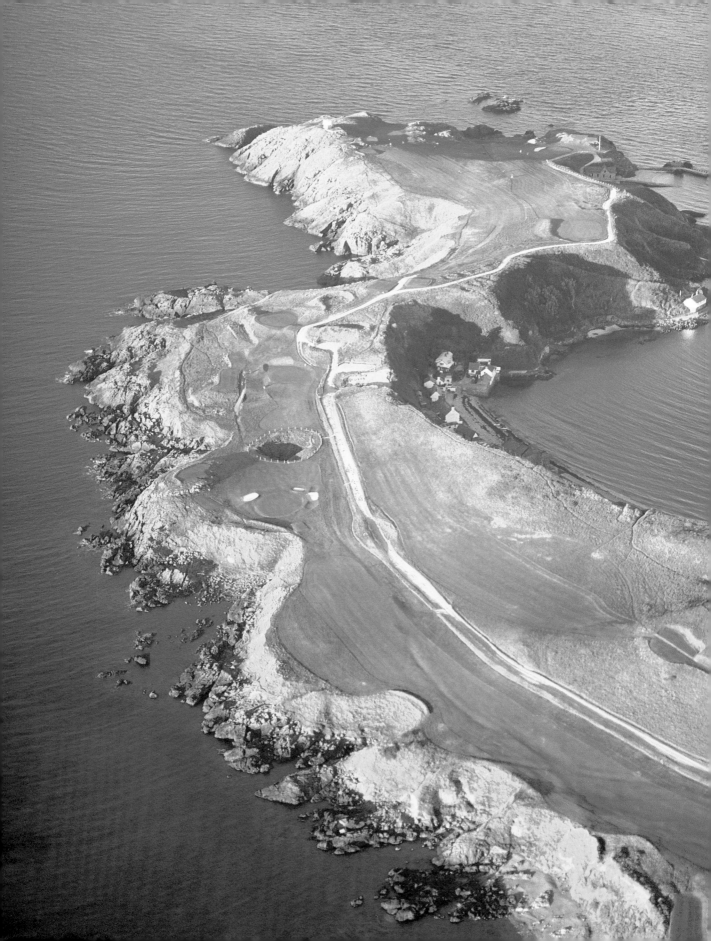

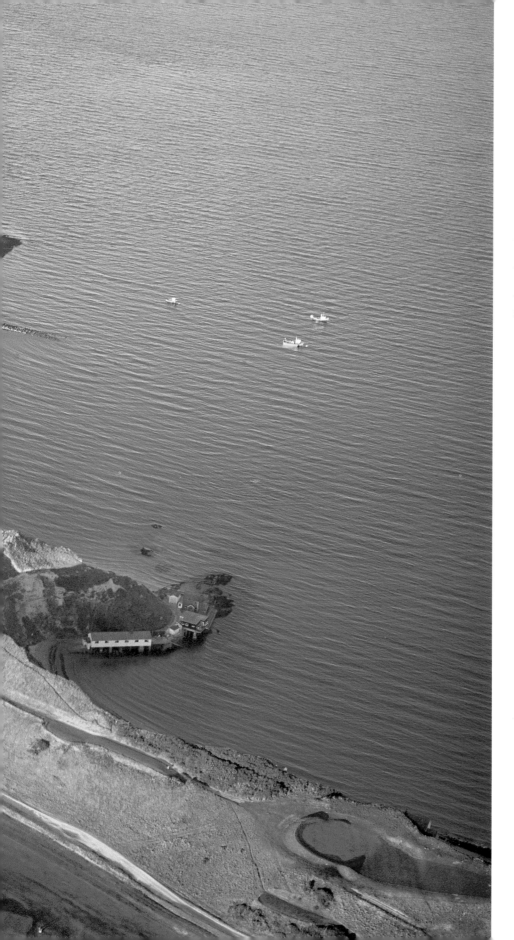

Porthdinllaen
On this dramatic promontory – its rocks and cliffs populated by seals and seabirds, and designated a Site of Special Scientific Interest – you will find a former fishing village, archaeological sites, coastguard and lifeboat stations – and the spectacular clifftop course of Nefyn Golf Club. From the National Trust car park for Porthdinllaen, at Morfa Nefyn, follow the track through the golf course to the little village on the beach – the Tŷ Coch Inn provides sustenance.
Photographer, David Williams.

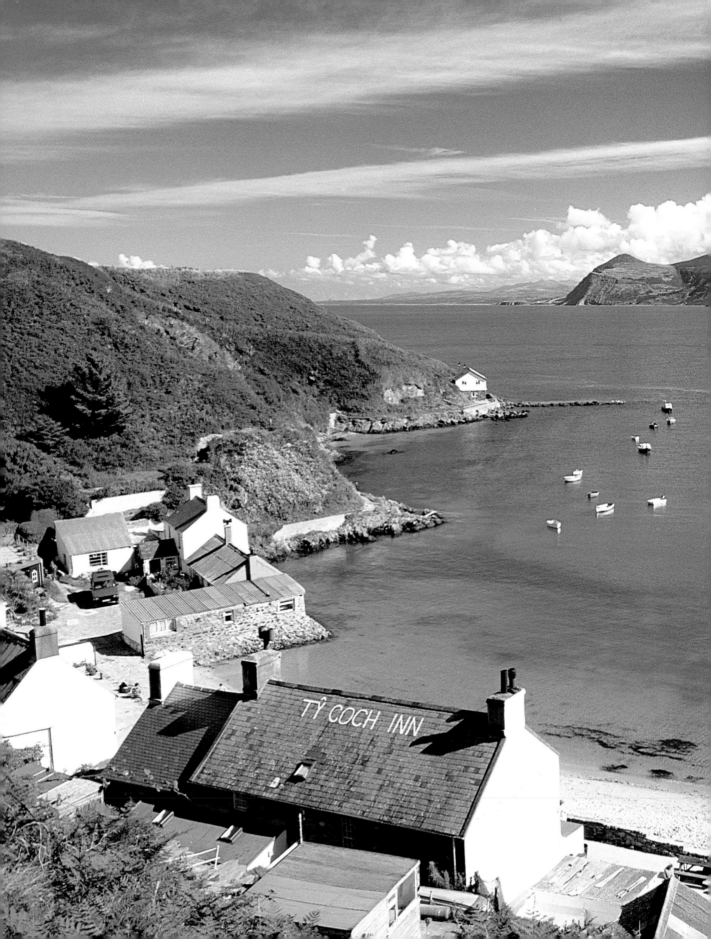

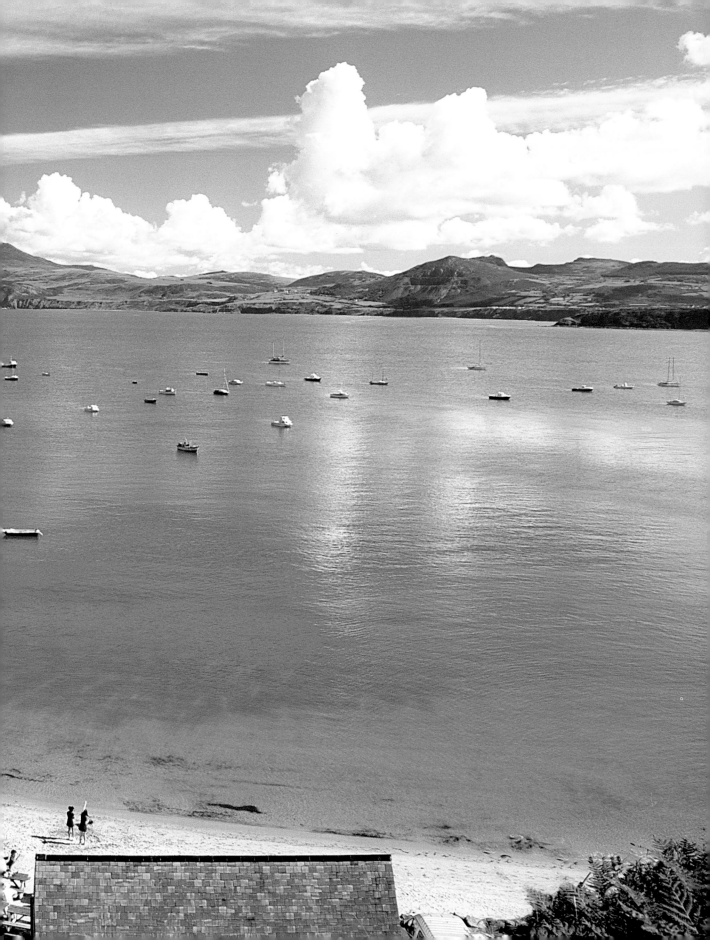

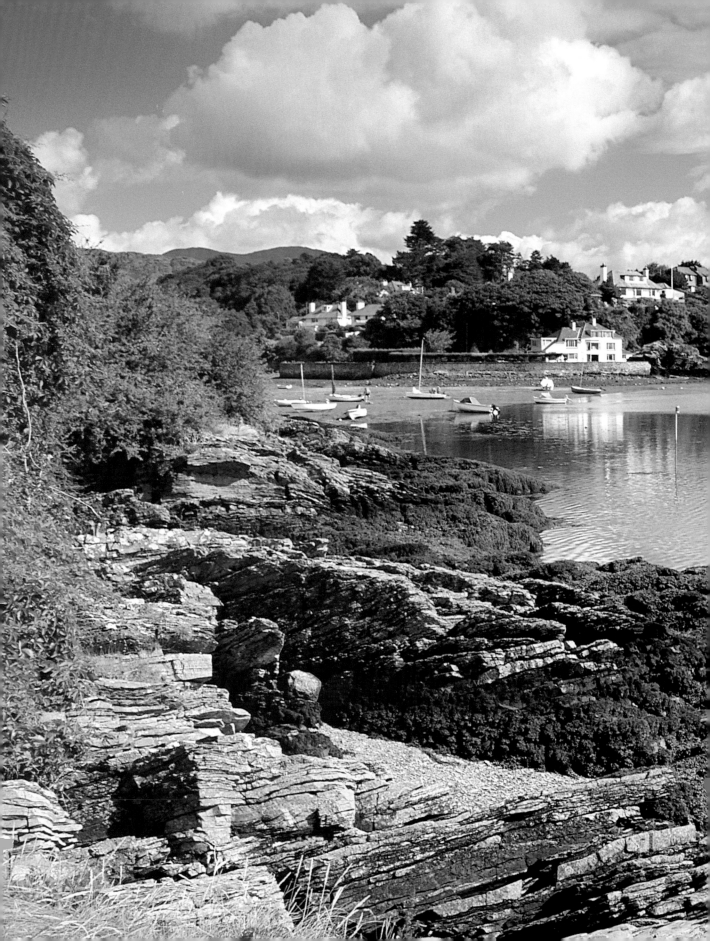

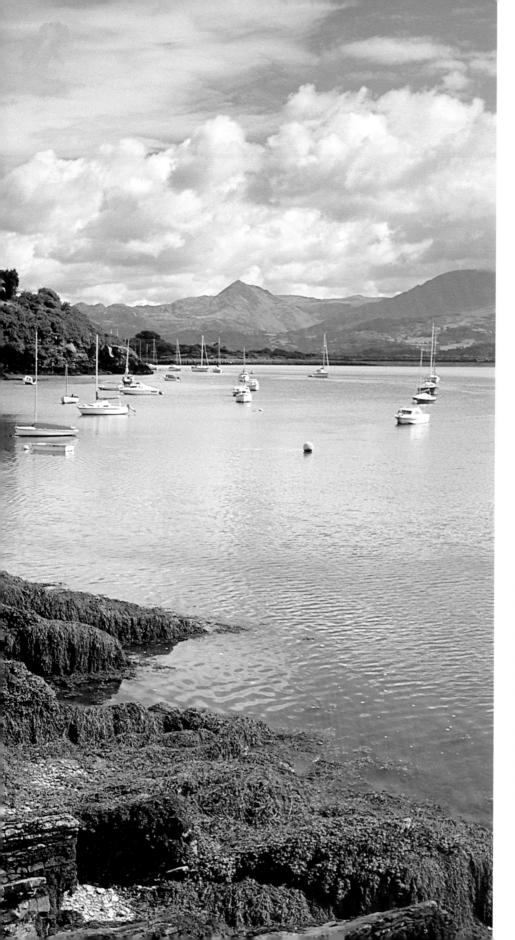

Porthdinllaen and The Rivals
Pages 34/35
The three summits of The Rivals – each of which can appear the highest, depending on where you are – dominate the view across the bay from Porthdinllaen. The National Centre for Language and Culture at Nant Gwrtheyrn, in their shadow, is the place to learn Welsh in incomparable surroundings. Explore the Llŷn Heritage Coast path – a well-marked route linking bays, cliffs and headlands along 112 miles of shoreline listed as an Area of Outstanding Natural Beauty.
Photographer, Dave Newbould.

Borth y Gest
The captains of Porthmadog's 19th-century schooners – which carried Welsh slate to the world – built solid houses here, in which to enjoy well-earned retirement surrounded by souvenirs of their voyages. It remains a tranquil retreat away from the bustle of the nearby town. From Porthmadog, walk along the narrow road past Madoc Yacht Club to Borth-y-Gest and along the rocky coast westward – there are majestic views of Snowdonia across the estuary.
Photographer, Jeremy Moore.

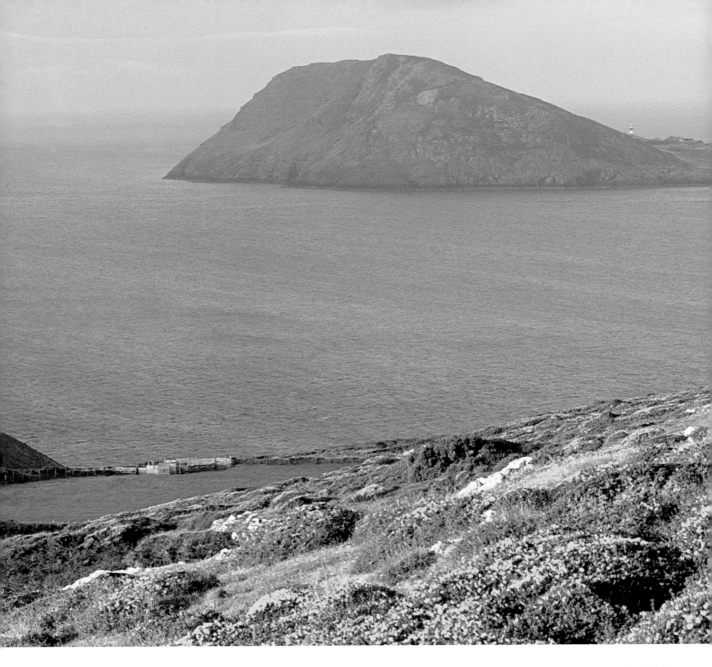

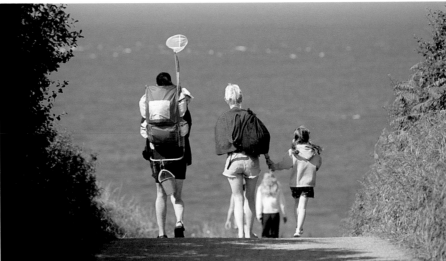

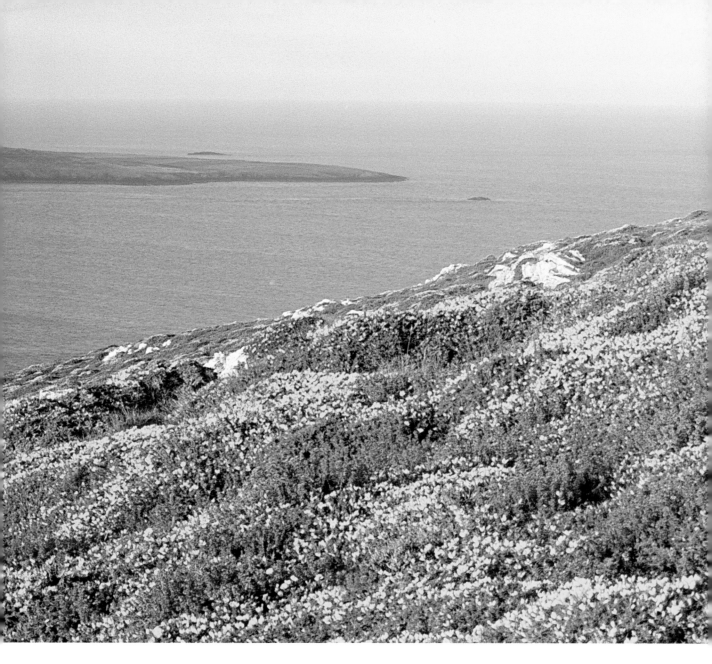

Whistling Sands
This family has all the essentials for a great day at the beach – bucket and spade, gift-shop fishing net for investigating rock pools – and, no doubt, picnic, drinks and sun lotion. Whistling Sands is named for the squeaking sound made by the coarse sand if you shuffle through it. The uncrowded beaches at Tudweiliog, Porth Ysgaden, Porth Colmon and Porth Oer are all worth a visit – they are all on the Llŷn Heritage Coast footpath.
Photographer, Steve Benbow.

Bardsey Island
Mystical Bardsey has long been a place of pilgrimage – three journeys here equalled one to Rome. In settled weather, when the tide is right, it is possible to cross by boat from Aberdaron, where clergyman R. S. Thomas channelled his concern for the landscape and culture of Wales into powerful poetry. Follow the Pilgrim's Route, which links the churches and holy wells of Llŷn – maps are available from churches and local shops.
Photographer, Steve Benbow.

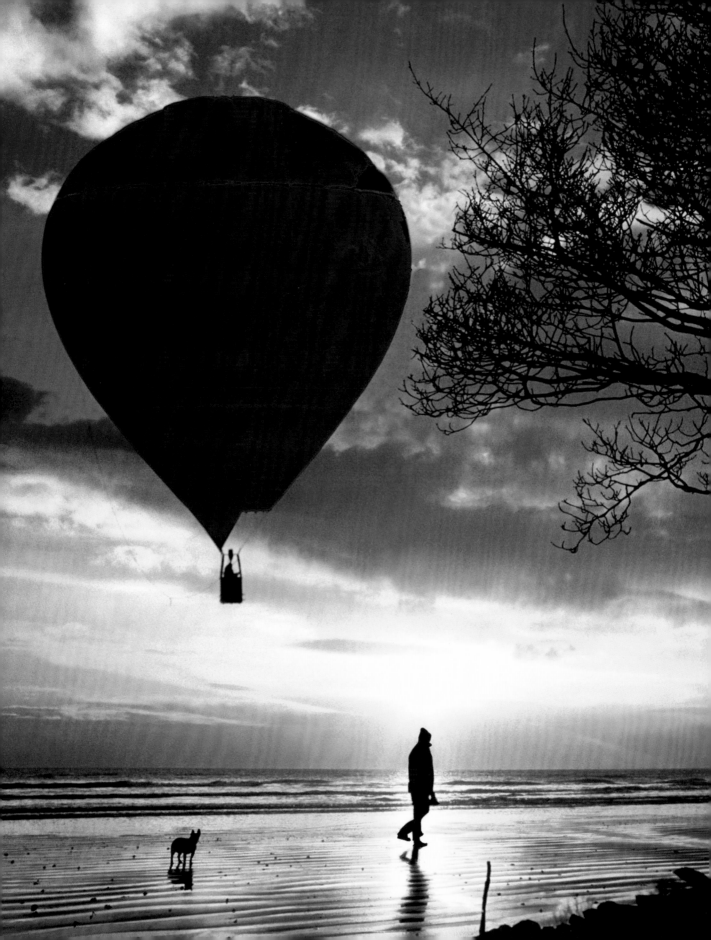

Black Rock Sands

This vast beach extending some three miles from Borth y Gest to Criccieth – with views of southern Snowdonia – gives a tremendous feeling of limitless sea and sky. Walk along this or any other westward-facing beach in Wales for a profound sensation of smallness under scudding clouds or fiery sunset.
Photographer, Steve Peake.

Portmeirion

The visionary architect Clough Williams-Ellis searched Britain for a landscape in which to set his imaginative ideas – and found it on his own doorstep in Wales. Portmeirion, his entertaining Italianate village, charms with carefully aligned vistas that place exotic inspirations against a Welsh backdrop. Leave the A487 at Minffordd, across the estuary from Porthmadog, and enter another world – imagine yourself on a Mediterranean shore, or helping 1970s television hero The Prisoner plot his escape from the village.
Photographer, David Williams.

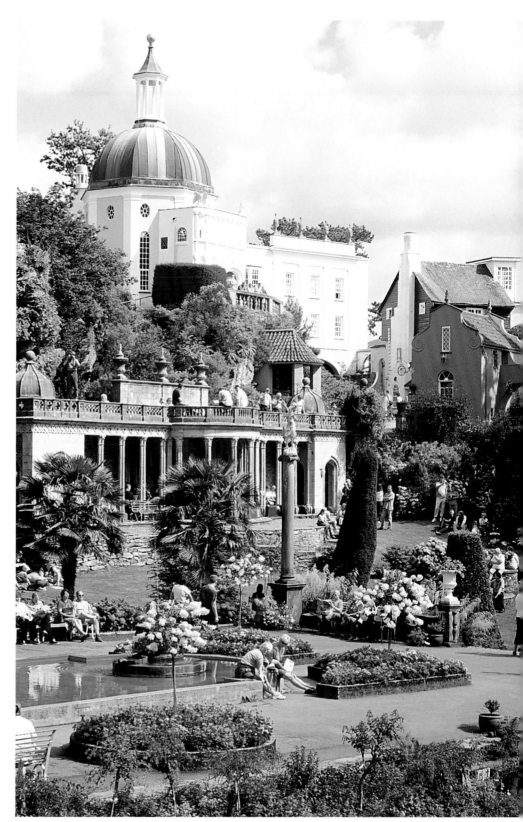

Conwy Valley

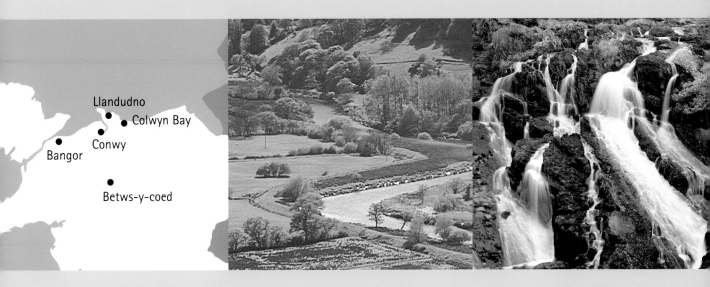

The River Conwy and its tributaries run through a landscape which is gentler and more wooded than the bare upland of Snowdonia to the west.
In its lower reaches, the Conwy meanders lazily along its valley before opening out into a broad tidal estuary, as it makes its way to the sea.

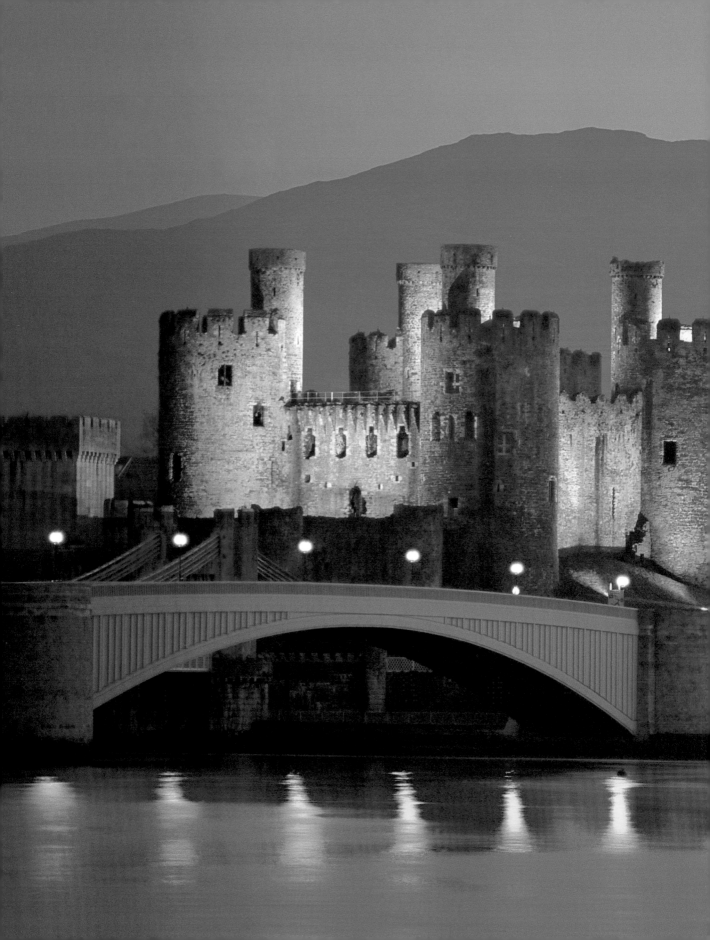

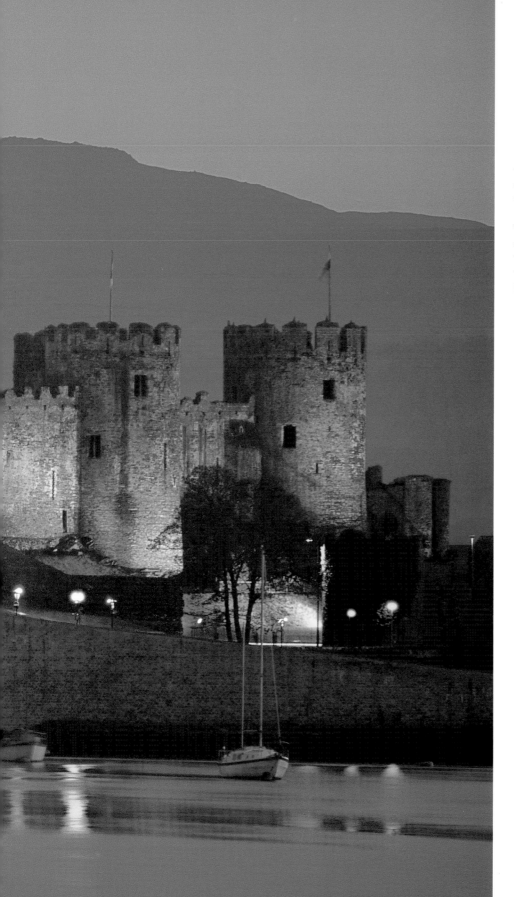

Conwy Castle
Built by Edward I, Conwy Castle is one of a ring of castles that includes Caernarfon, Beaumaris and Harlech. Together, as the finest examples of medieval castles and fortified town walls in the UK, they form a UNESCO World Heritage Site. Visit the castle, but be sure also to walk the town walls for great views over Conwy to the estuary and harbour. Photographer, Pierino Algieri.

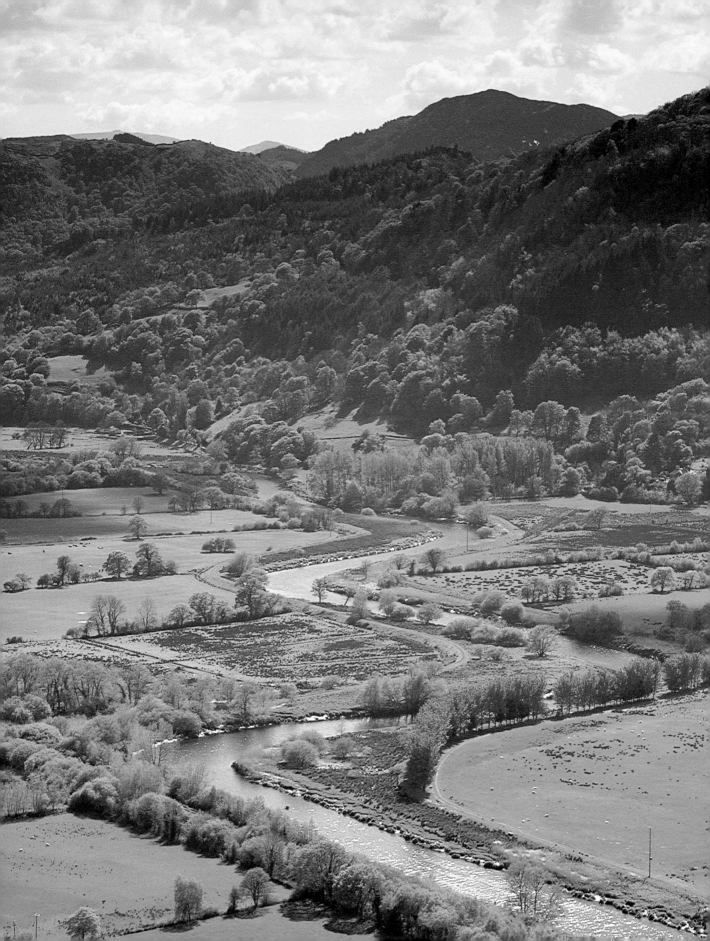

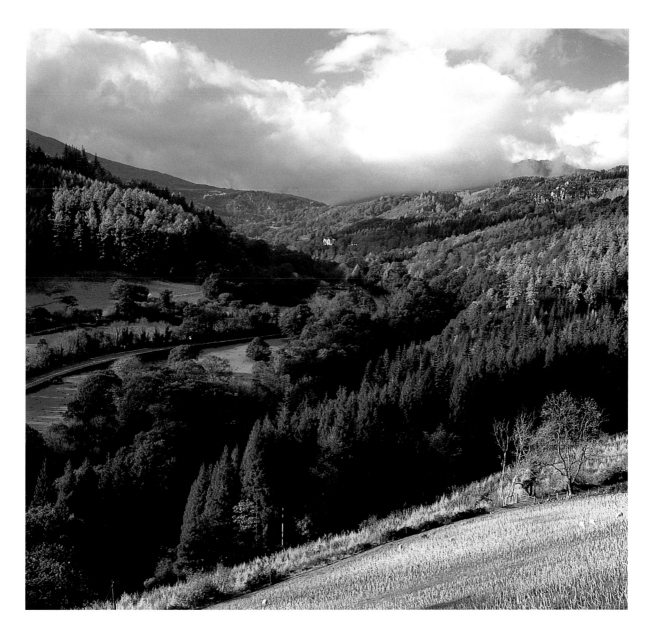

Conwy Valley near Trefriw
The floor of the Conwy Valley is fertile farmland, while the slopes bordering Snowdonia are fine walking and mountain-biking country. At Trefriw, iron-rich water, from springs discovered by the Romans, supplies a health-giving spa – and water-driven generators power a woollen mill. Highlights of the lower Conwy Valley include the woollen mill at Trefriw and Bodnant Garden, one of the very best in Wales.
Photographer, Dave Newbould.

Forestry, near Betws-y-coed
Large tracts of upland Wales are given over to commercial forestry. Where once the policy was to plant blocks of a single species, the trend is now toward growing a variety of trees in more natural-looking plantations. Many forest tracks are open to walkers and cyclists, and the Forestry Commission runs some excellent campsites – tourist information centres have details.
Photographer, Jeremy Moore.

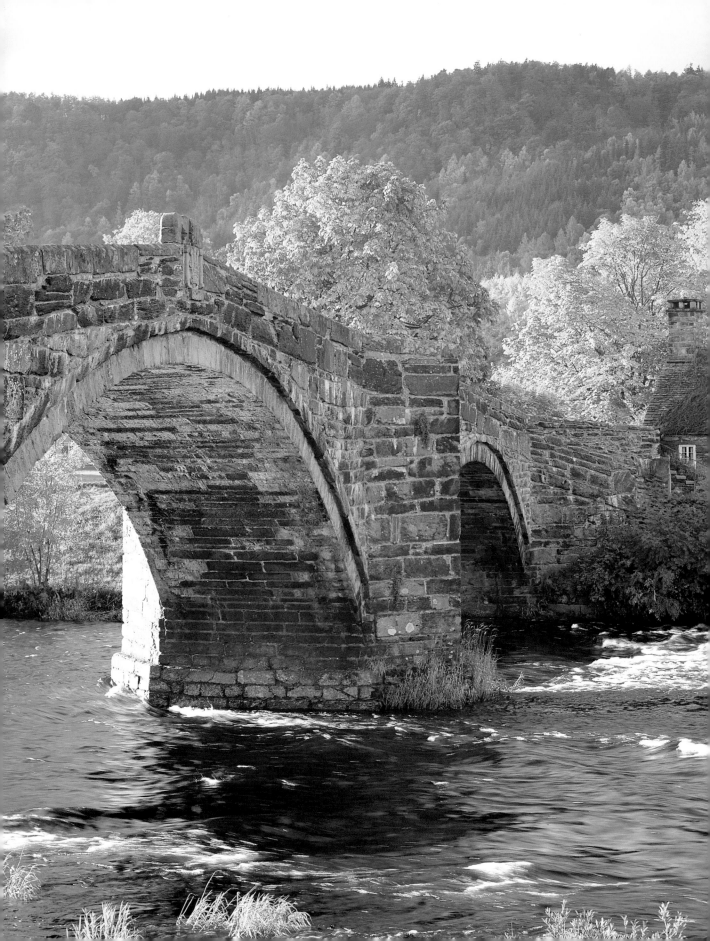

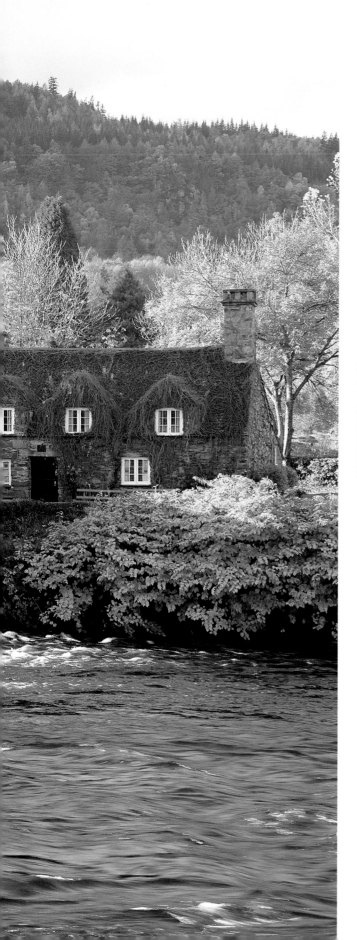

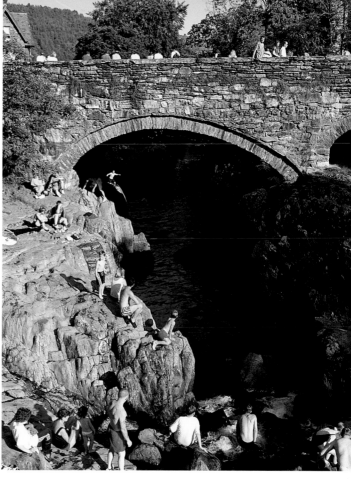

Llanrwst

The market town of Llanrwst, in its pastoral setting of villages and farms, seems all the more delightful in contrast to the commanding presence of Snowdonia's peaks. The narrow bridge is believed to have been designed by Inigo Jones for the Wynn family of Gwydir Castle. Walk, or drive carefully, over the bridge and across the valley to visit Gwydir Castle, an early Tudor courtyard house skilfully restored to its former glory.
Photographer, Chris Warren.

Betws-y-coed

Once a stop on the old coach road from London to Holyhead, and a popular resort in Victorian times, Betws-y-coed is accustomed to crowds. It can become very busy on summer weekends, when the temptation to cool off near the river is understandable. Walk for a few minutes along the riverside paths and you will soon find yourself in peaceful surroundings. A trail for wheelchair users heads into the forest just west of Betws-y-coed.
Photographer, Steve Benbow.

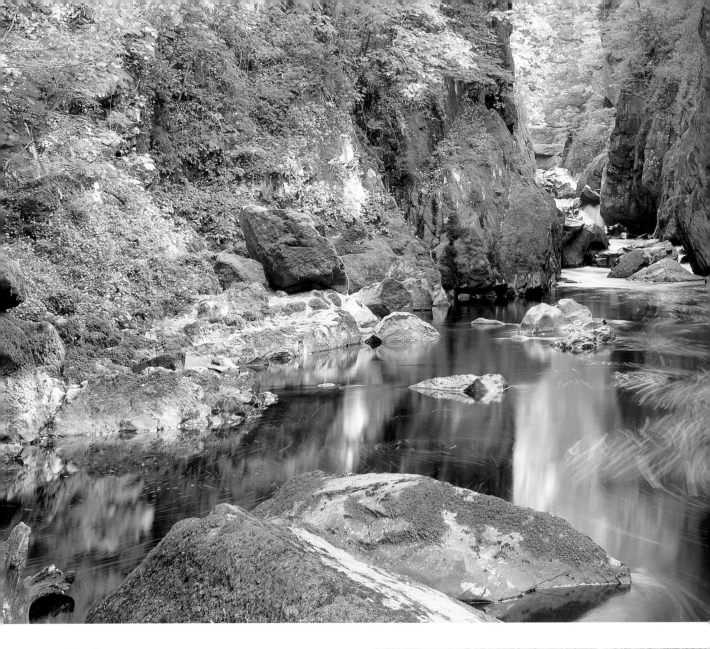

Fairy Glen
This remarkable chasm, and the Conwy Falls just upstream, were on the itinerary of every Victorian traveller to Snowdonia. The birthplace of Bishop William Morgan, whose translation of the Bible into Welsh secured the survival of the language, is at nearby Penmachno. Combine a walk to the Fairy Glen with a visit to Tŷ Mawr Wybrnant, Bishop Morgan's home, now in the care of the National Trust. Photographer, Paul Kay.

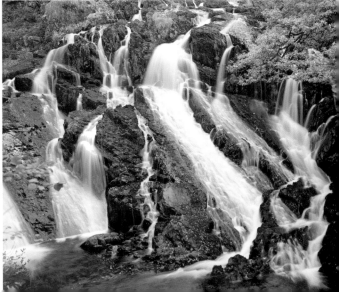

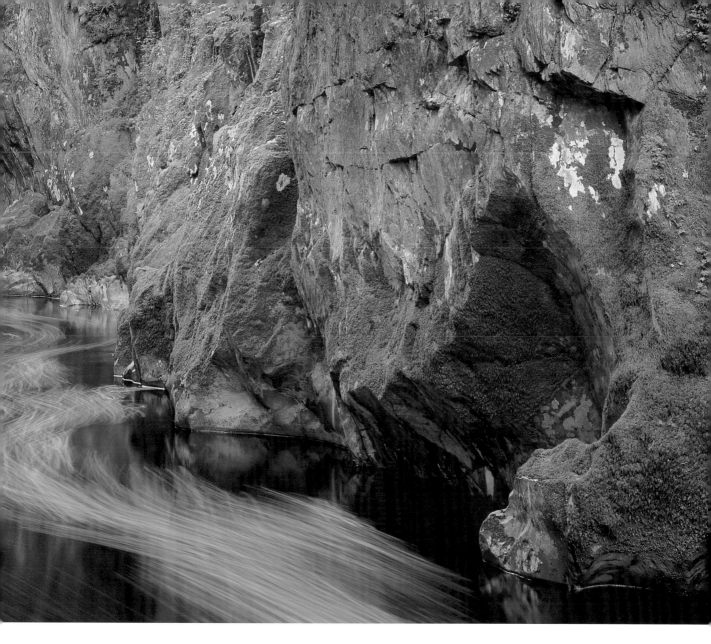

Swallow Falls

The River Llugwy rushes down these spectacular falls before joining the Conwy at Betws-y-coed. The attractive town has hotels, cafes, craft shops, tourist information centre and a railway museum. Photographer, Chris Gallagher.

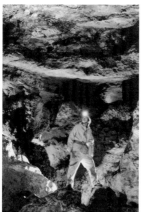

Great Orme

The limestone outcrop of Great Orme dominates Conwy Bay. The world's largest Bronze Age mining remains, where copper ore was extracted 4,000 years ago, extend 150ft below the surface and are open to visitors from February to October. Drive high above the sea on the giddying road from Llandudno Pier to the West Shore. Or visit the summit of Great Orme by cable-car in one direction and Victorian tramway in the other. Photographer, Steve Peake.

Vale of Clwyd

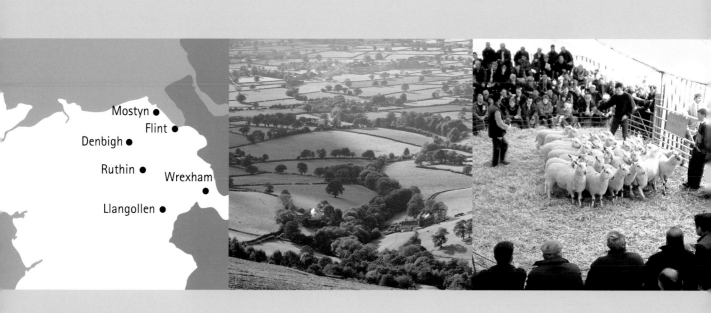

There are regions of Wales where the importance of agriculture manifests itself strongly. The wide Vale of Clwyd, viewed from the hills above, gives an impression of burgeoning productivity – of farmers dispersing their produce through the market towns of Ruthin and Denbigh to the wider population.

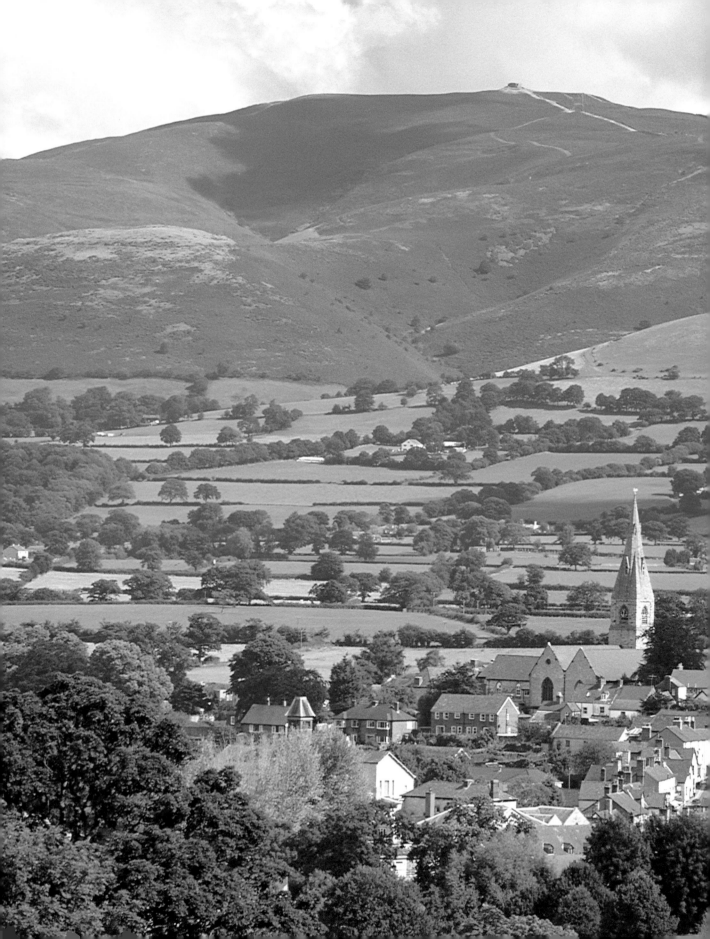

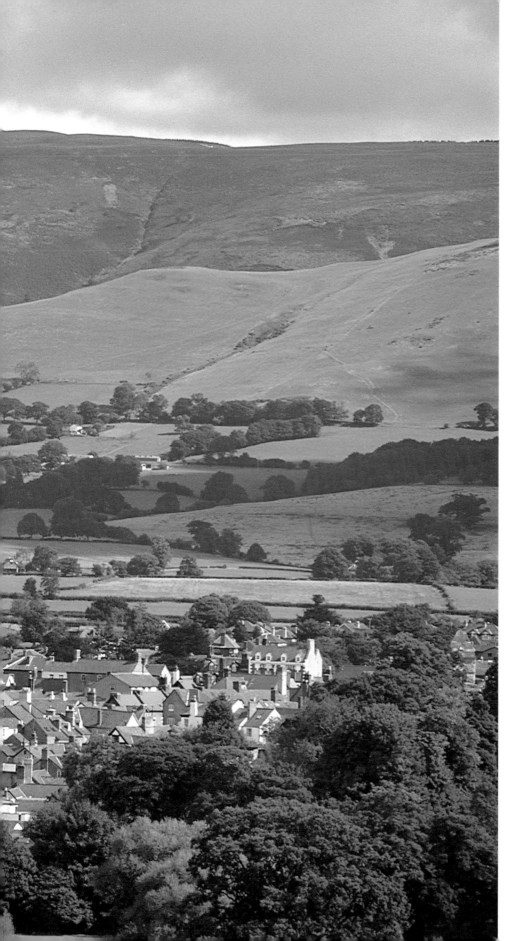

Ruthin

Overlooked by Moel Famau and the Clwydian hills, Ruthin is an ancient market town and commercial centre that has long served the Vale of Clwyd. Ruthin's buildings reward a close look – from Ruthin Castle to the hilltop town centre with its church, old prison, ancient pubs and half-timbered buildings. Photographer, Dave Newbould.

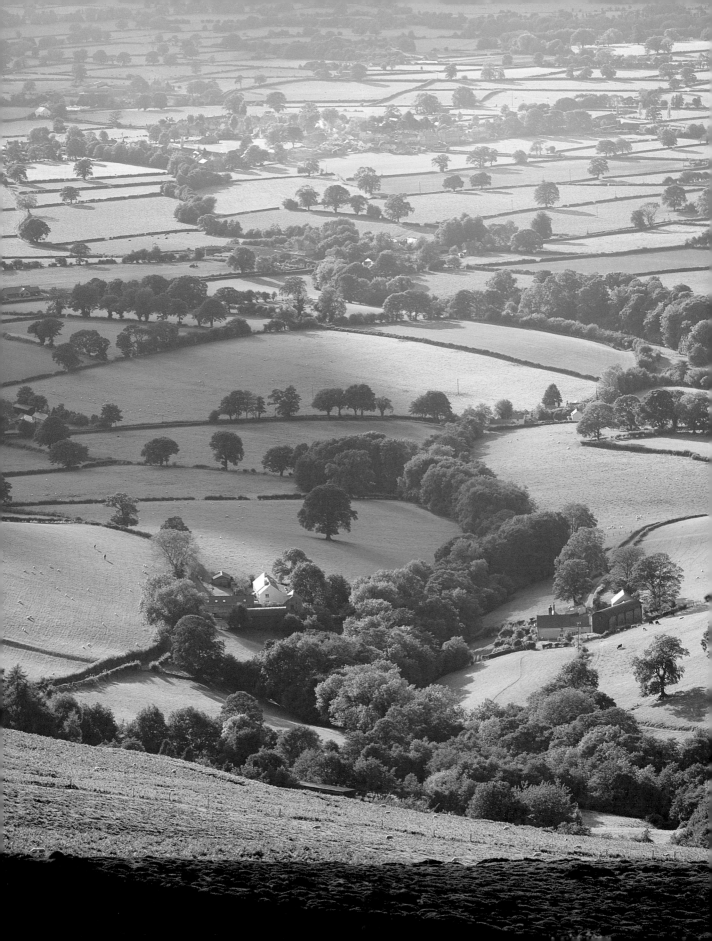

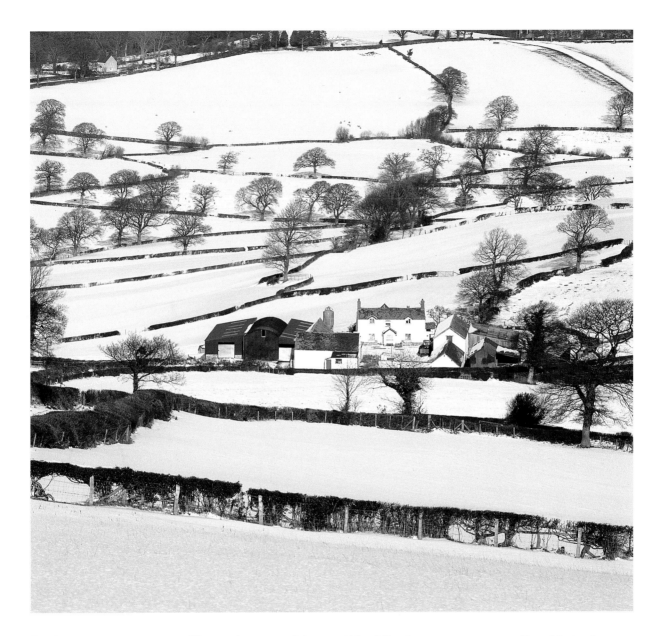

Farming

Hill farms tend to be widely spaced, as the poor-quality land will not support a high density of livestock, while the valley floor supports more intensive agriculture. A thriving Welsh-language cultural life keeps people in touch. Take a drive along the A525 – which links Ruthin, Denbigh and St Asaph, the smallest cathedral city in the UK – to gain a sense of the scale of the farming economy. Photographer, David Woodfall.

Vale of Clwyd

Winter transforms the vale into a carpet of white, criss-crossed by stone walls and punctuated here and there by the welcoming homeliness of a farmhouse. The farmers must work on regardless, especially when the first lambs make their appearance. Rug Chapel, an elaborately decorated private chapel, and Llangar Church, a rustic parish church, are delightful examples of contrasting ecclesiastical styles, just west of Corwen. Photographer, David Woodfall.

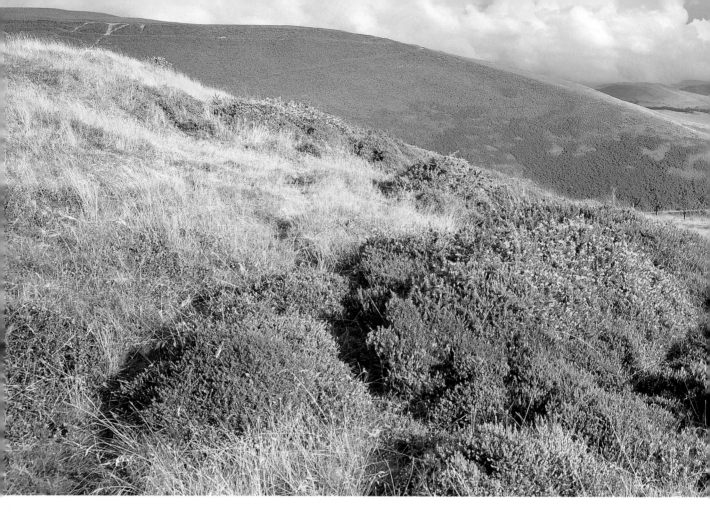

Clwydian Hills

The Clwydian range includes this region's most significant summit, Moel Famau, at 1,820ft. The Offa's Dyke long-distance footpath traverses these hills before descending to the coast at Prestatyn. Visit Loggerheads Country Park to learn about the natural history and industrial heritage of Flintshire. Or head for the summit of Moel Famau for tremendous views of the Vale of Clwyd, from uplands to sea. Photographer, David Woodfall.

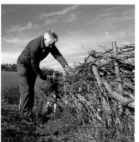

Corwen, hedge laying

Traditional skills remain essential where the terrain rules out large-scale industrial farming. Agricultural colleges still teach centuries-old methods. Erddig Hall and the Clywedog Valley near Wrexham, and the Greenfield Valley near Flint, are good places to visit for an understanding of social and industrial history. Photographer, Geraint Wyn Jones.

Wrexham, sheep auction

The auctioneer calls out rapid volleys of prices as sheep are paraded in the ring and buyers decide how high they will bid – a scene repeated many times a week throughout Wales. Look out for the famers' produce markets, which are an increasingly popular way of buying directly from the source – or visit the covered market in Wrexham. Photographer, Steve Peake.

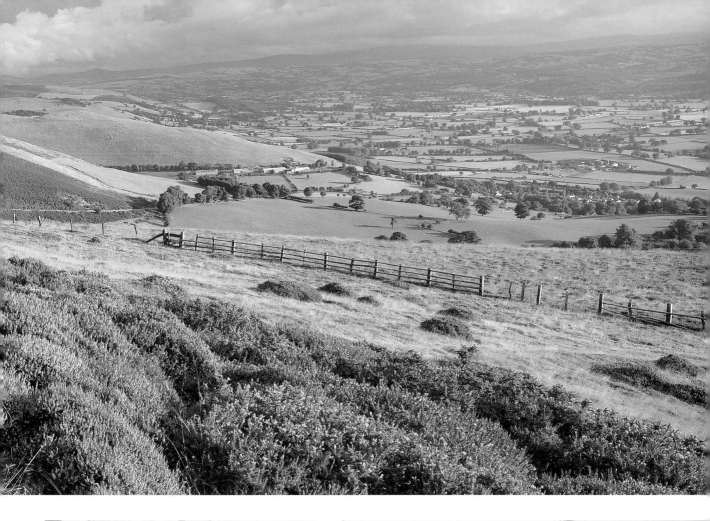

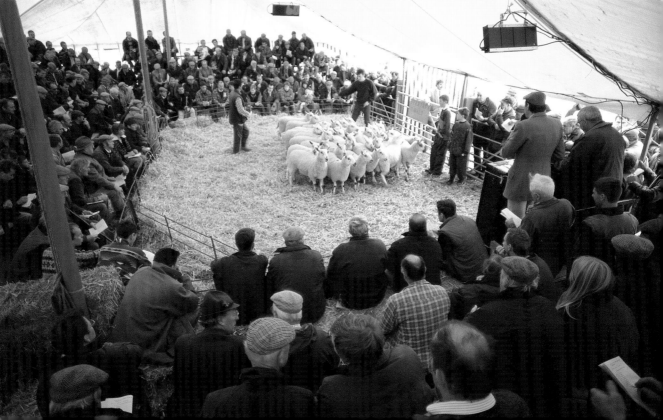

Llangollen and the Dee

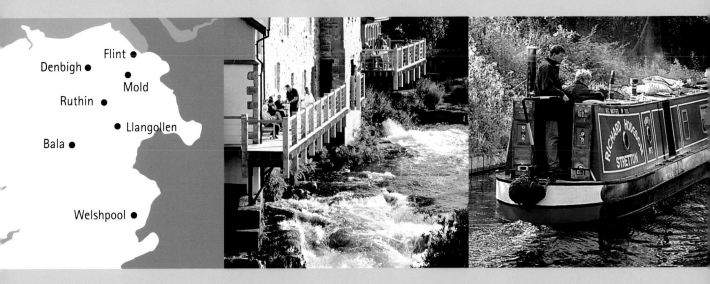

Llangollen, tourism capital of north-eastern Wales, delights on many levels. The town is lulled by the sound of the river and echoes to the tooting of steam trains. The sylvan surroundings of Valle Crucis Abbey contrast with the bareness of the Horseshoe Pass and Eglwyseg Mountain.

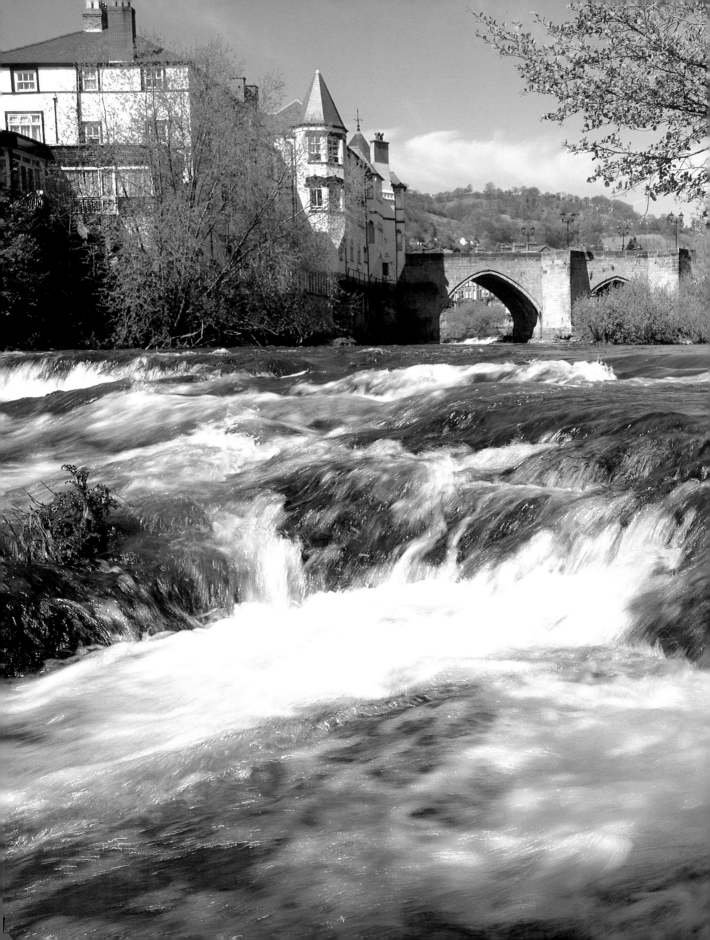

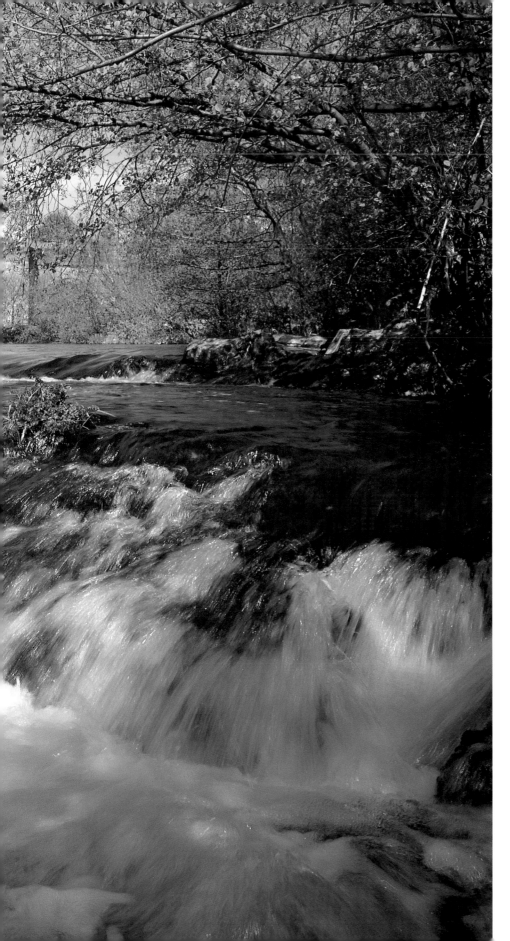

Llangollen

The rocks that force the Dee to thunder past, over impressive rapids, also provided the best place to build a bridge across the river – enabling the town to grow in its scenic setting. Llangollen lends itself to exploration by walking – signposted paths to the banks of the Dee, and to other attractions, radiate from the town centre near the bridge. Photographer, David Williams.

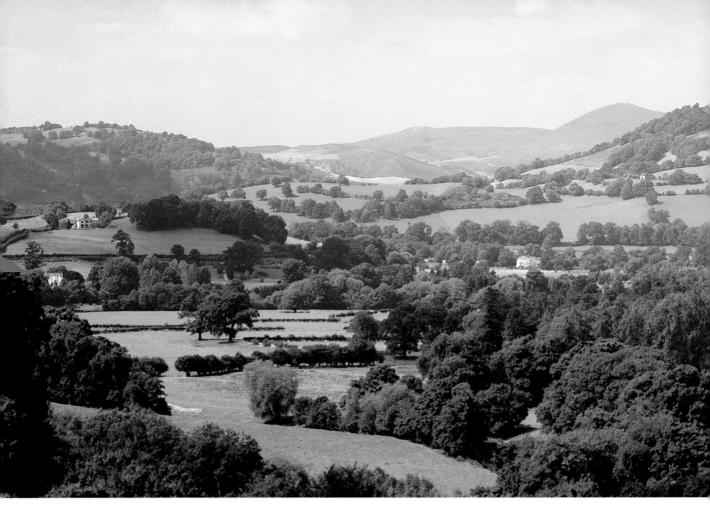

The Vale of Llangollen

Having collected several tributaries since leaving Bala Lake, the Dee is a substantial river by the time it reaches the Vale of Llangollen. Attractions in the region include the Llangollen Canal, Chirk Castle and the ruin of Castell Dinas Brân, visible for miles around on its distinctive hilltop. From Llangollen, drive to Chirk and its castle, stopping to view the Froncysyllte aqueduct on the way – then continue to Llanarmon Dyffryn Ceiriog, which has won many best-kept village awards. Photographer, Chris Gallagher.

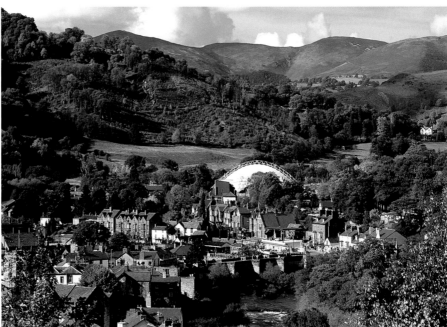

Photographer, Dave Newbould.

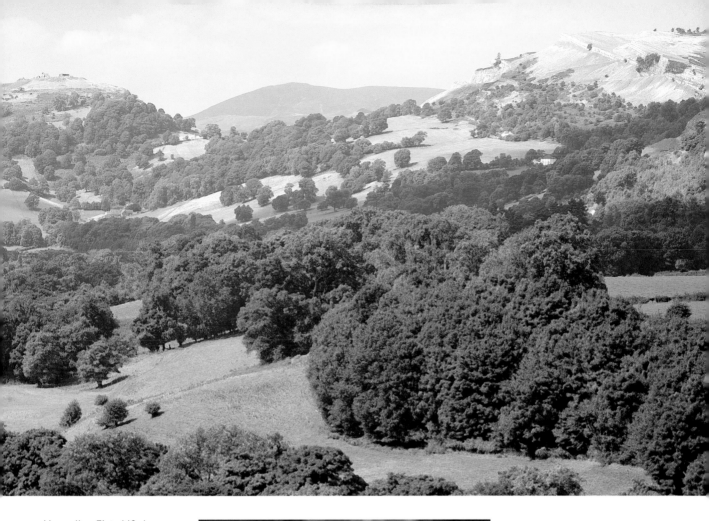

Llangollen Eisteddfod
The people of the town welcome the world each summer as they host gifted singers, instrumentalists and dancers at the Llangollen International Musical Eisteddfod. Visit during the first week of July to experience the friendly atmosphere and high musical standards of the Eisteddfod – or check the programme for world-music events held throughout the year. Photographer, David Williams.

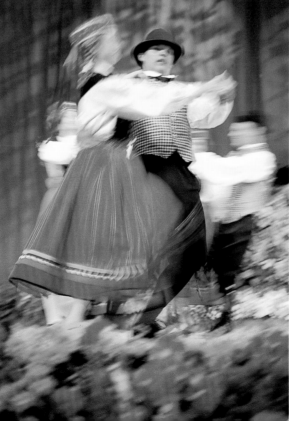

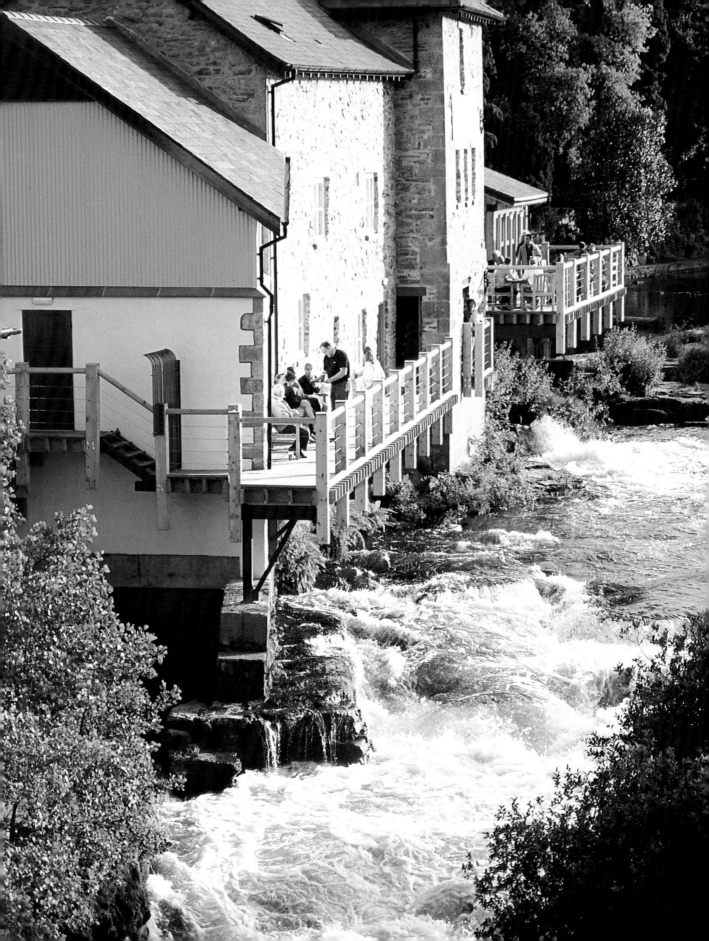

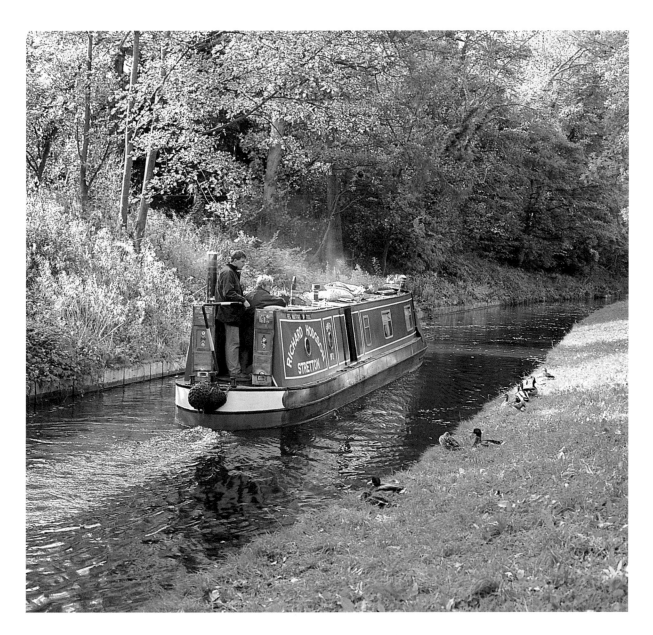

The Corn Mill
Llangollen has many pubs
and restaurants, including
this former water mill which
overlooks the Dee in
spectacular fashion. Fortify
yourself to explore the region
at one of the wide range of
eating places – from cosy
pubs to sophisticated hotels.
Photographer, David Williams.

Llangollen Canal
Generally agreed to be
the most scenic canal in
the entire UK network,
the Llangollen Canal heads
eastward from the town
and is carried high above the
River Dee by the Froncysyllte
and Chirk aqueducts. There
are horse-drawn canal boat
trips from Llangollen – or
you could navigate the canal
on a hired narrowboat.
Photographer,
Geraint Wyn Jones.

Lakes and waterfalls

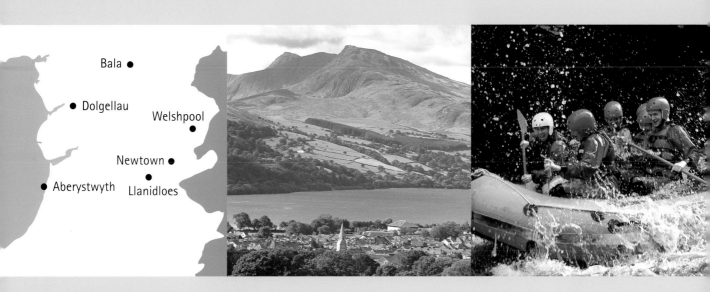

Bala ●

● Dolgellau
Welshpool
●

Newtown ●
●
● Aberystwyth   Llanidloes

The wide swathes of mountain and moorland that form central Wales are lightly populated, but they are put to good use for agriculture, forestry and for supplying water – a commodity of which, it must be said, this elevated landscape receives an abundant supply.

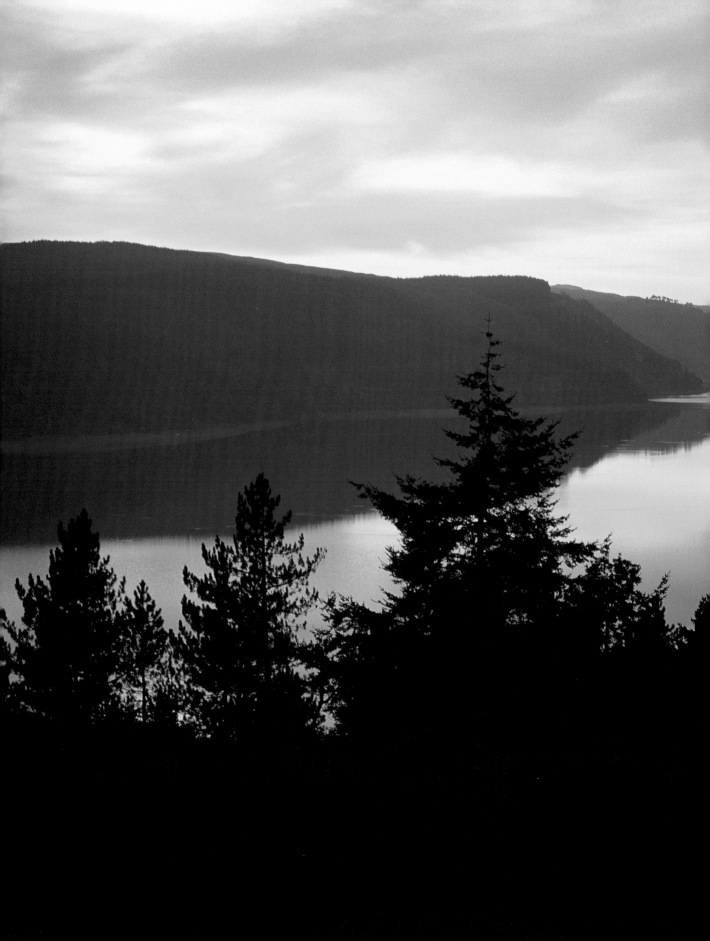

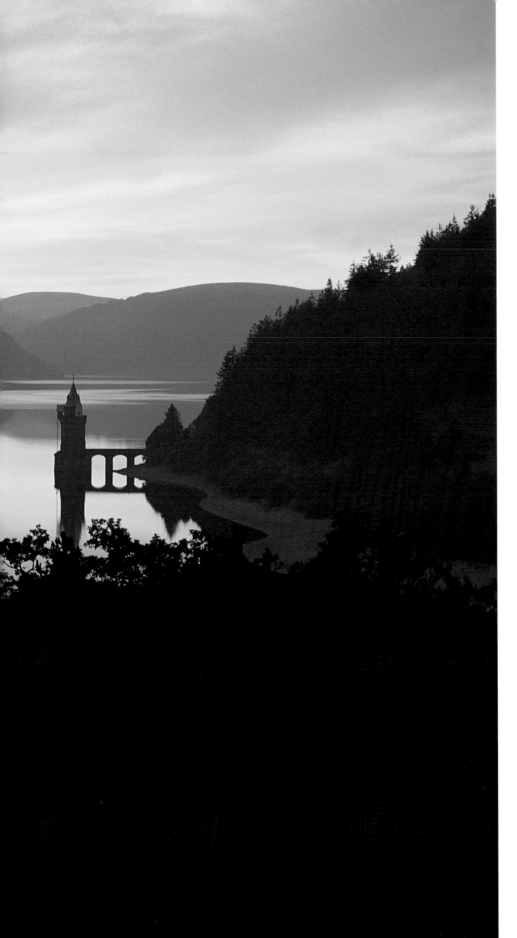

Lake Vyrnwy
Several of the largest lakes in Wales are reservoirs. Lake Vyrnwy's pumping station, with its Victorian Gothic tower, lends a hint of Switzerland to the scene. The Lake Vyrnwy Hotel has boats for hire, with electric outboards that do not pollute the water – and you will usually find someone at the bar willing to dispense good fishing advice.
Photographer, David Williams.

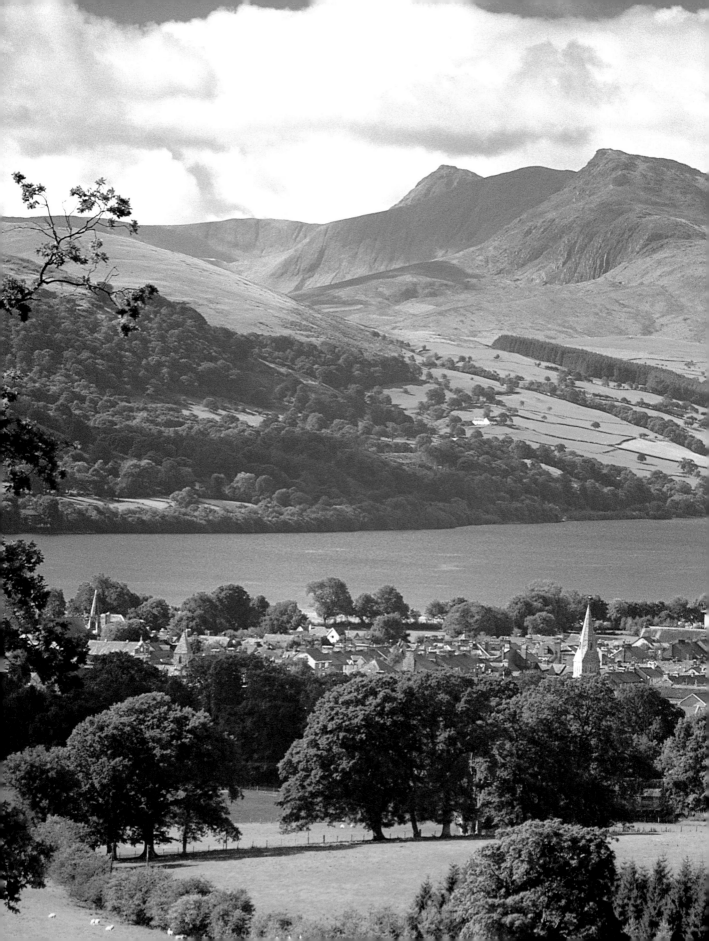

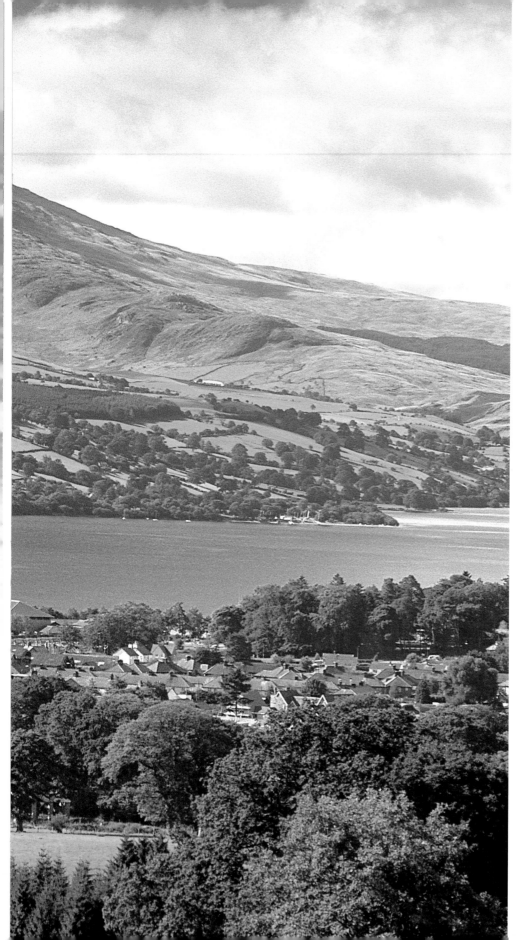

Bala Lake
Extending from the town of Bala at its outflow to the Aran mountains in the distance, this is the largest natural lake in Wales. It is home to a species of fish, the Gwyniad, that has been marooned here since the last Ice Age. Take in the scale of the lake and the surrounding mountains by boarding the Bala Lake Railway for a trip to Llanuwchllyn via Llangower. Photographer, Dave Newbould.

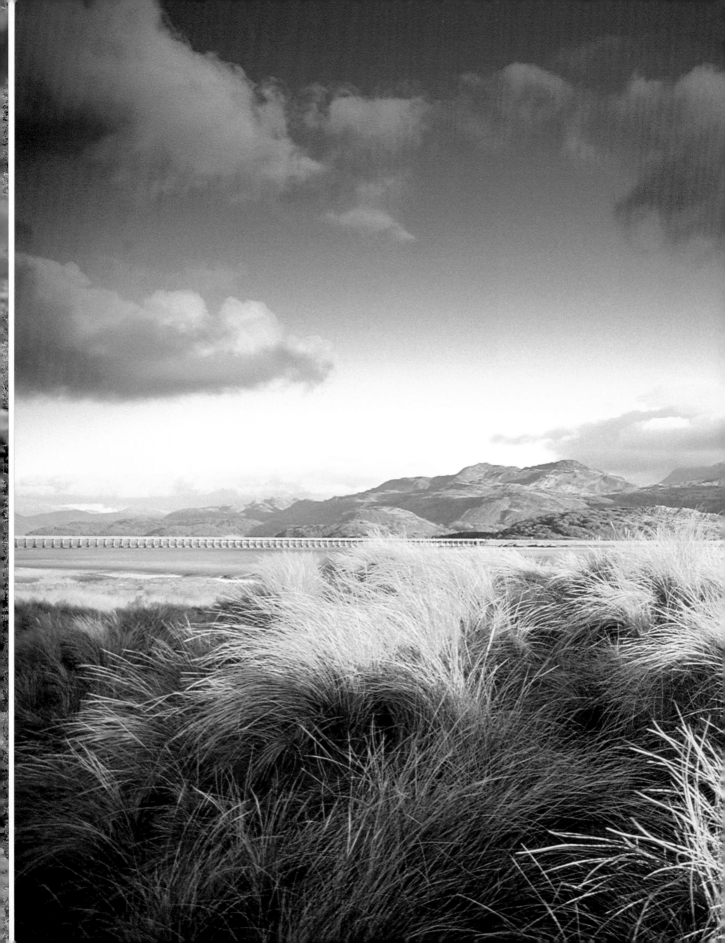

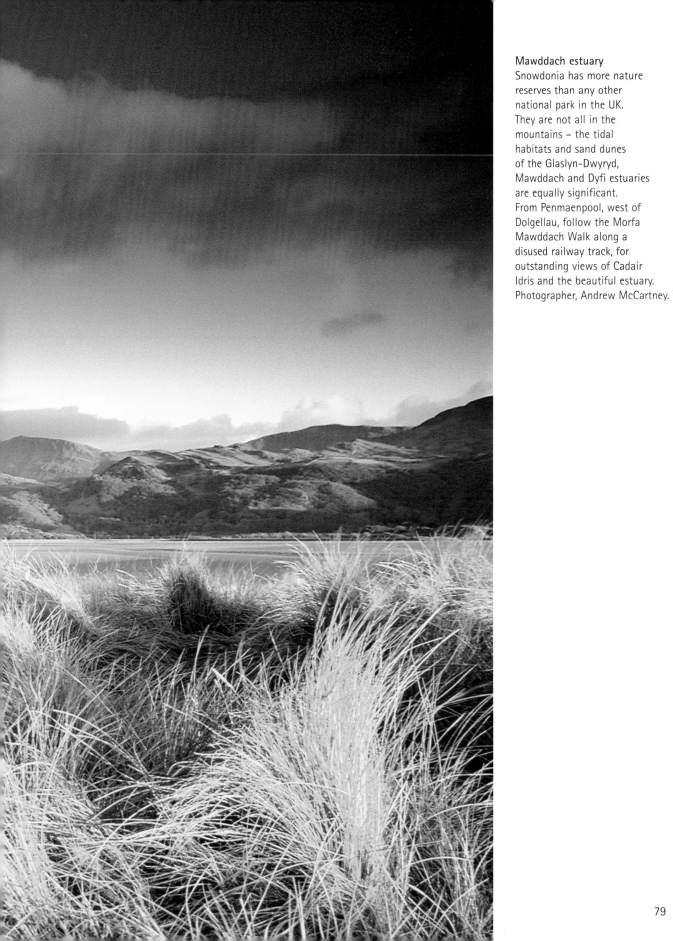

Mawddach estuary
Snowdonia has more nature reserves than any other national park in the UK. They are not all in the mountains – the tidal habitats and sand dunes of the Glaslyn-Dwyryd, Mawddach and Dyfi estuaries are equally significant. From Penmaenpool, west of Dolgellau, follow the Morfa Mawddach Walk along a disused railway track, for outstanding views of Cadair Idris and the beautiful estuary. Photographer, Andrew McCartney.

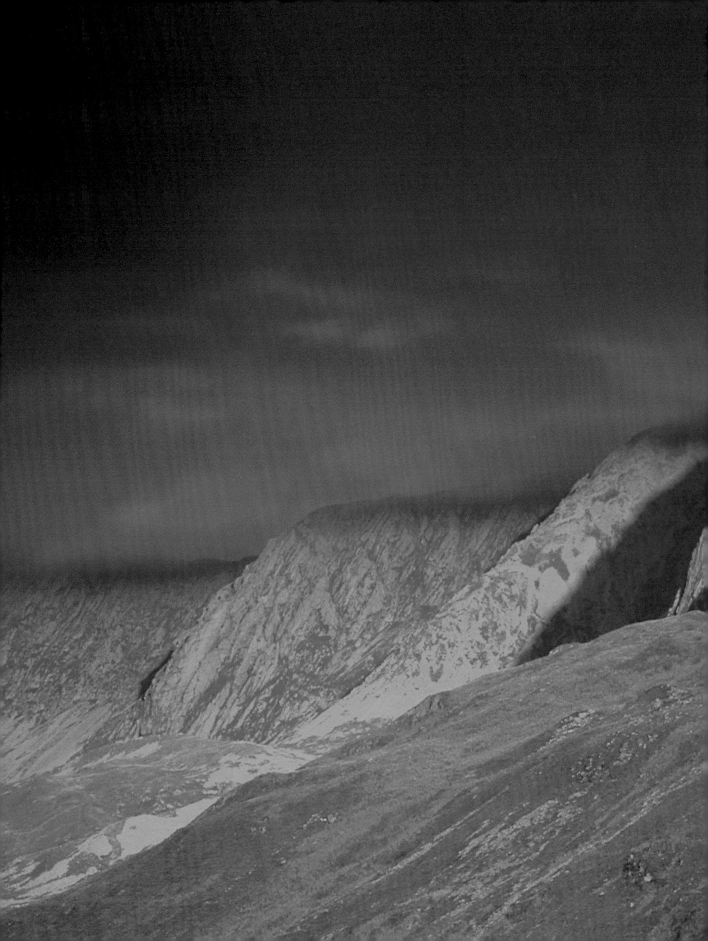

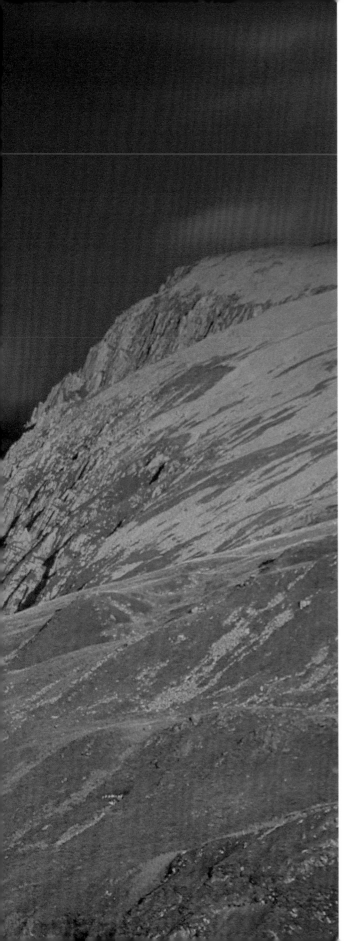

Cadair Idris
This 2,927ft mountain dominates the views from Dolgellau and the Mawddach estuary. Legend has it that anyone who spends a night on the summit will wake up blind, mad or a poet. From Arthog, follow a narrow road to Llynnau Cregennen and enjoy views of Cadair Idris across the lakes. The climb to the summit is strictly for experienced mountain walkers.
Photographer, Dave Newbould.

Llyn Cynwch
This lake near Dolgellau is just one of many in Wales to provide excellent fishing in inspiring surroundings. Llyn Cynwch is on the route of the Precipice Walk, signposted from Dolgellau, which gives magnificent views to all points of the compass – the less energetic might find the lake a pleasant place to wait for others tackling the whole circuit.
Photographer, David Williams.

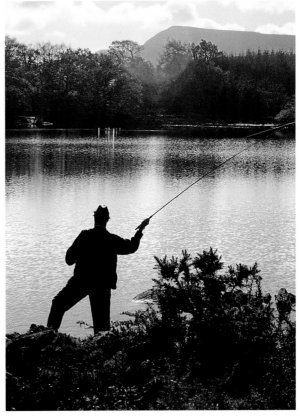

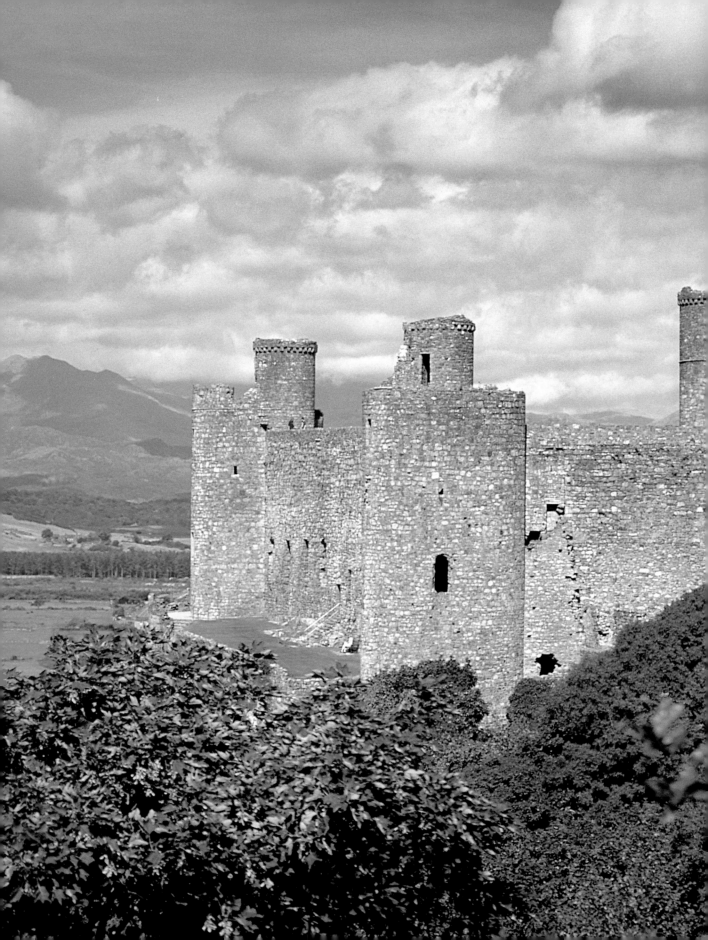

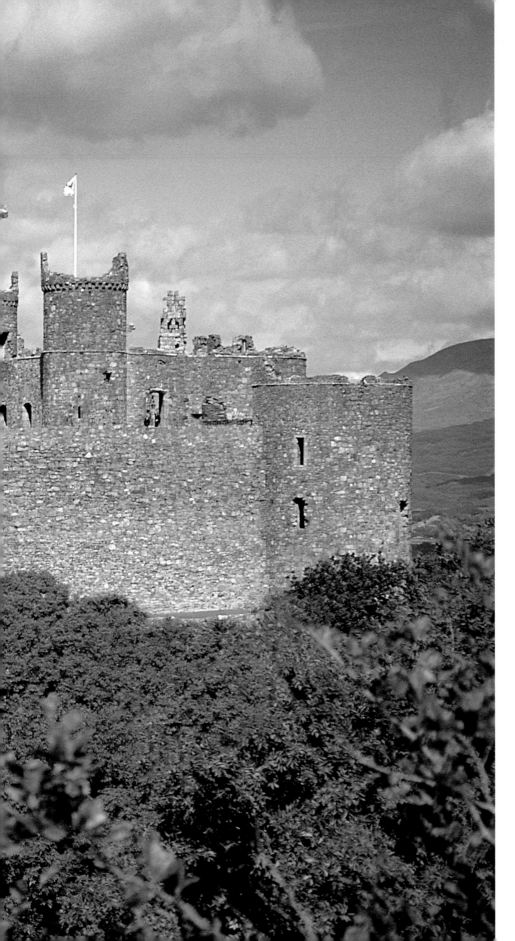

Harlech Castle

Designed to appear intimidating from both land and sea, Harlech Castle seems to grow out of the rock outcrop on which it stands. Built for Edward I, it was also used as a base by Owain Glyndŵr. A siege during the Wars of the Roses inspired the stirring song 'Men of Harlech'. A walk around the lofty battlements gives panoramic views of Snowdonia and Llŷn – the local battle re-enactment society gives exciting and informative presentations in the castle each summer. Photographer, Dave Newbould.

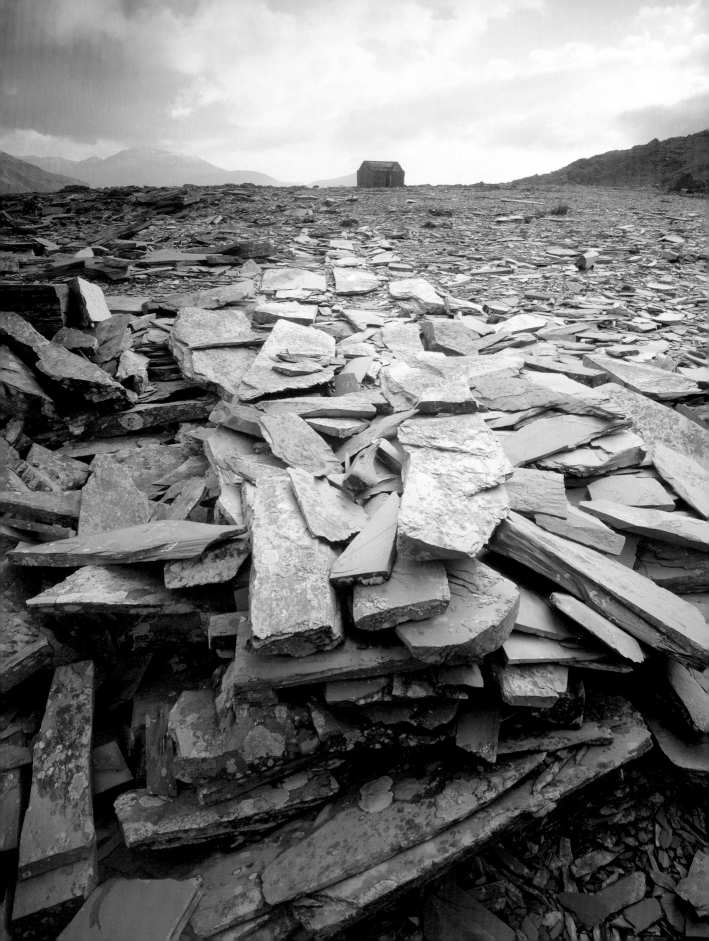

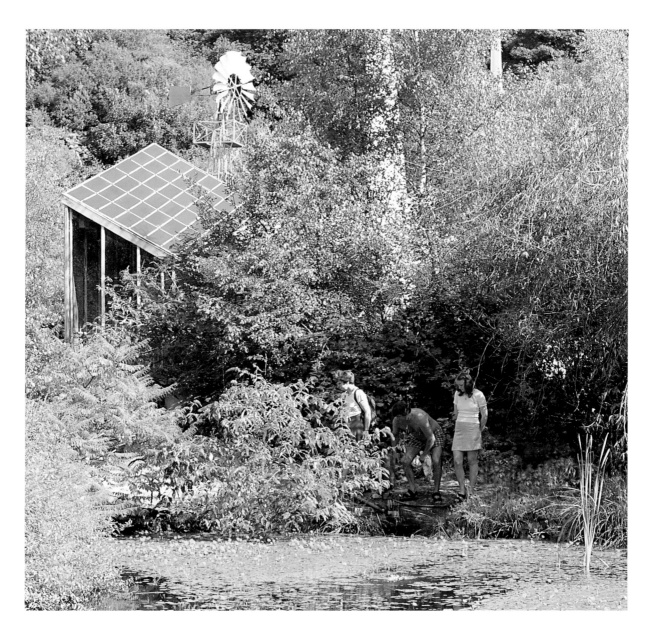

Cwm Croesor
Thousands of workers once laboured in the slate quarries and mines of Bethesda, Llanberis, Blaenau Ffestiniog and Corris. Production continues today, using modern methods – this versatile material is used in building, roofing, insulation and household products. The underground tours at Llechwedd Slate Caverns, Blaenau Ffestiniog and the Welsh Slate Museum at Llanberis both give insights into the lives of slate quarry workers. Photographer, Steve Peake.

Corris, CAT
The Centre for Alternative Technology, between Machynlleth and Corris, leads the way in developing environmentally friendly ways of using wind and water power, natural materials and traditional skills for the benefit of mankind. Head north from Machynlleth on the A487 to Pantperthog, where you will find this fascinating and highly educational centre. Photographer, Steve Benbow.

Rolling uplands

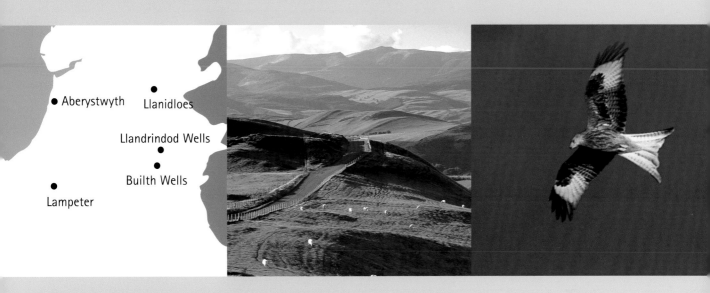

Aberystwyth Llanidloes

Llandrindod Wells

Builth Wells

Lampeter

From the high roads of mid Wales, ranges of hills extending to the horizon give the impression of an undulating ocean. The sources of our two longest rivers, the Severn and the Wye, are within a few miles of each other on the slopes of Plynlimon Fawr.

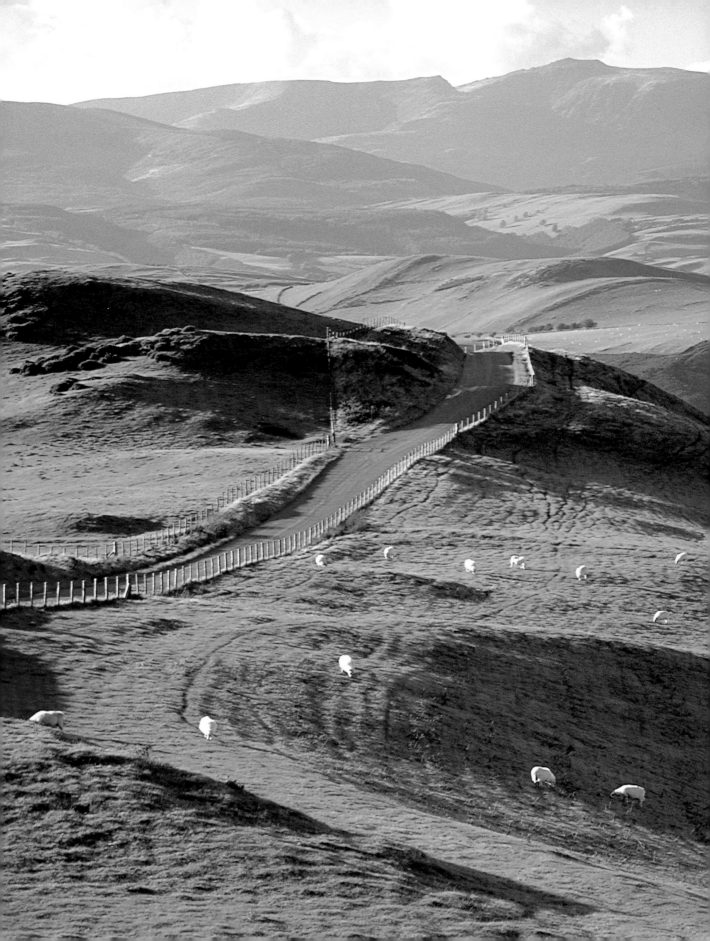

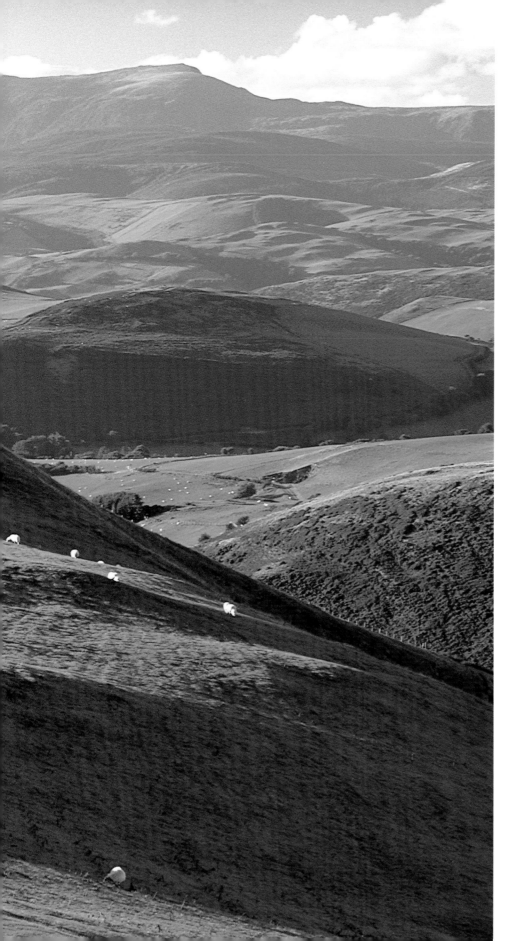

Meirionnydd
It is possible to drive the width of Wales here, from Cardigan Bay to England, in a couple of hours. Cultivated farming country alternates with remote and barren moorland, devoid of settlement for many miles. Explore Cwm Rheidol or Cwm Ystwyth and wonder at the determination of the people who lived by farming, and mining minerals, in these remote places.
Photographer, Jeremy Moore.

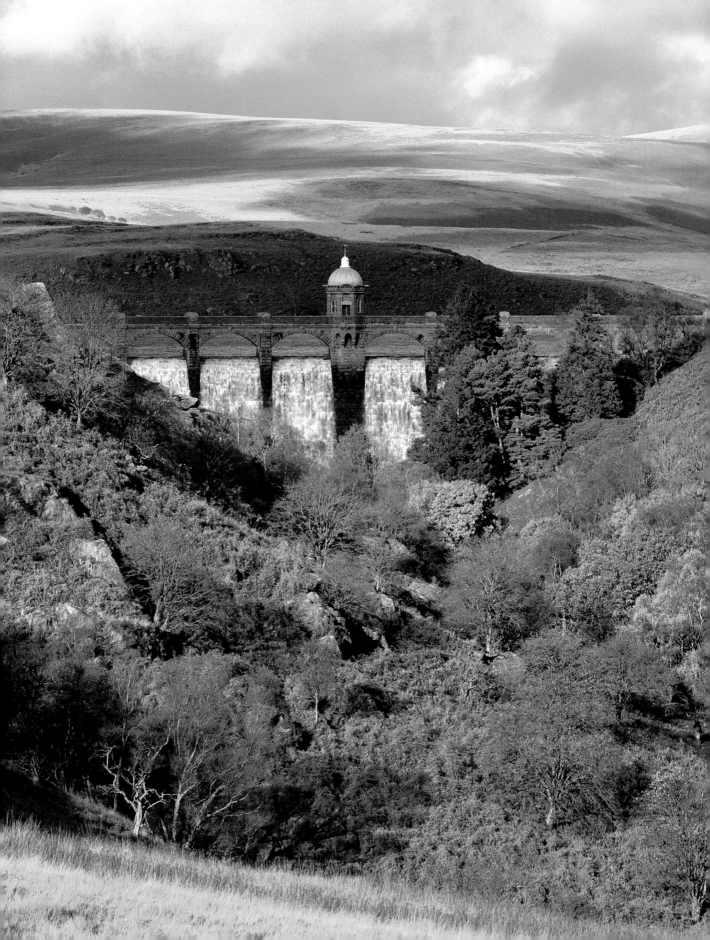

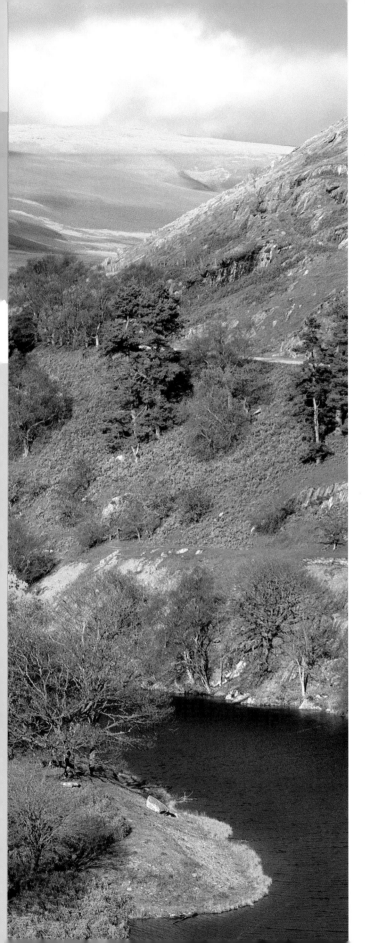

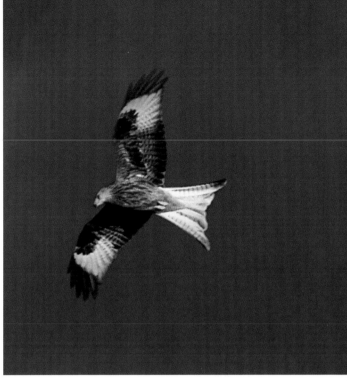

Elan Valley
Dominated by its impressive dam, this is one of several valleys in mid Wales where forestry and the supply of water are important activities. Seek out nature reserves, picnic sites and walking trails along the shores of the reservoirs, and in surrounding forests.
Photographer, Chris Warren.

Red Kite
Wales's largest bird of prey, once considered a pest, was reduced to the last few pairs in Britain here. In recent decades, with conservationists guarding nests, it has regained territory in mid Wales – several hundred pairs are steadily extending their range. Visit feeding centres at Rhayader, Bwlch Nant yr Arian (near Ponterwyd) or Tregaron to witness the supremely graceful flying skills of these remarkable birds, with their 5ft wingspan and long, forked tails.
Photographer, Jeremy Moore.

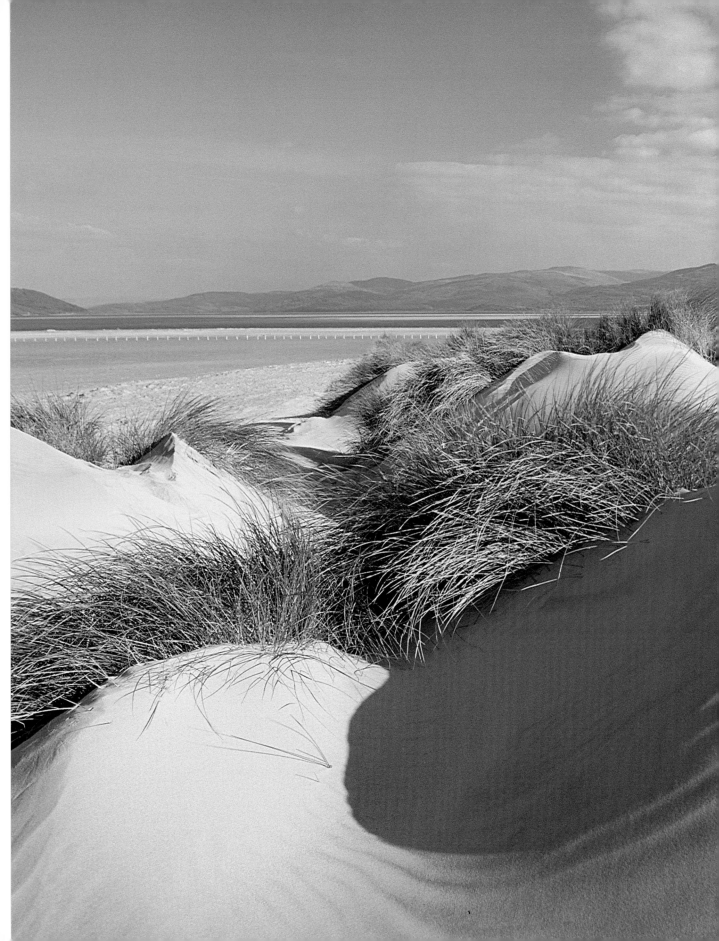

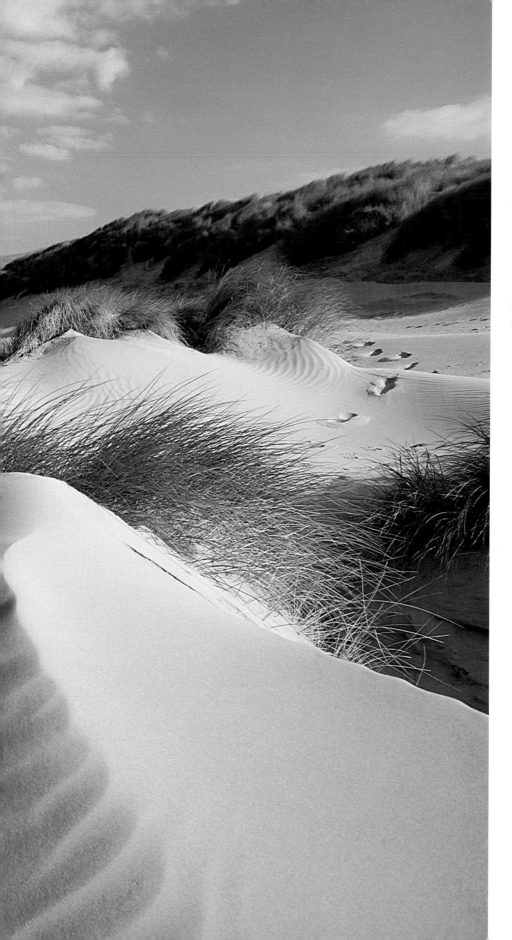

Ynyslas
Cardigan Bay was the UK's first Marine Heritage Coast, and has Special Area of Conservation status. These sand dunes at Ynyslas support seven species of orchid and are part of the Dyfi nature reserve, an important wintering site for wildfowl. The Ceredigion coast has everything from deserted sandy coves to bustling harbours of enormous character – with waterfront restaurants, welcoming hotels and guest houses, thriving yacht clubs and dolphin-spotting trips.
Photographer, Jeremy Moore.

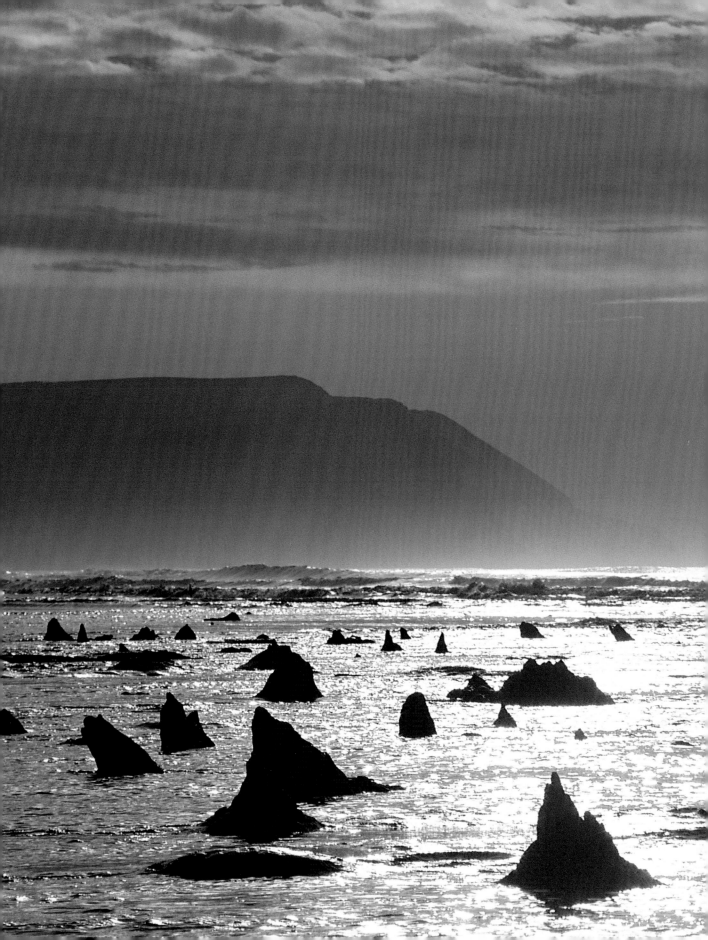

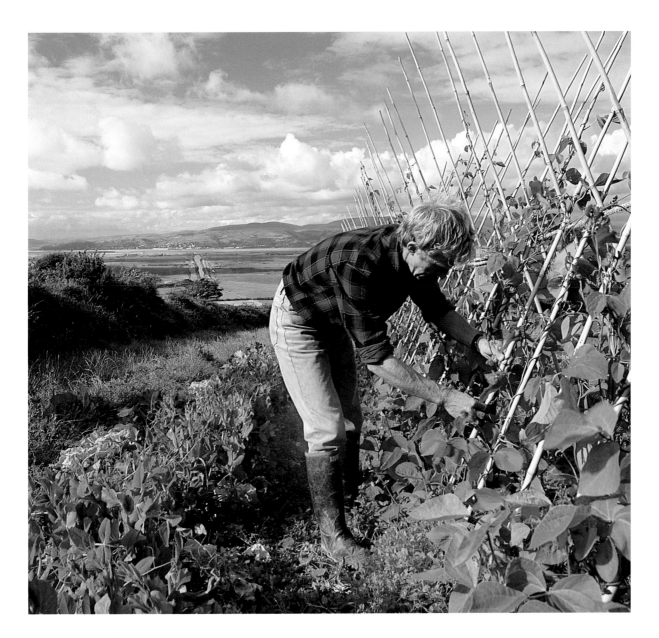

Borth, submerged forest
These remains of trees, revealed by the lowest tides, are evidence of change in the relative levels of land and sea. Cardigan Bay's three mysterious causeways, celebrated in legend as roadways to lost lands beneath the sea, are in fact moraines – lines of rock deposited by glaciers. Consult tide tables, or seek guidance locally, if you wish to follow the falling tide out to the submerged forest off Borth – head back to shore well before the tide turns. Photographer, Jeremy Moore.

Borth, organic farming
Many farmers in Wales opt to grow organic produce, often forming co-operative ventures to reach their customers. There are local agricultural shows throughout Wales during the summer months, with stands selling fine produce. Photographer, Jeremy Moore.

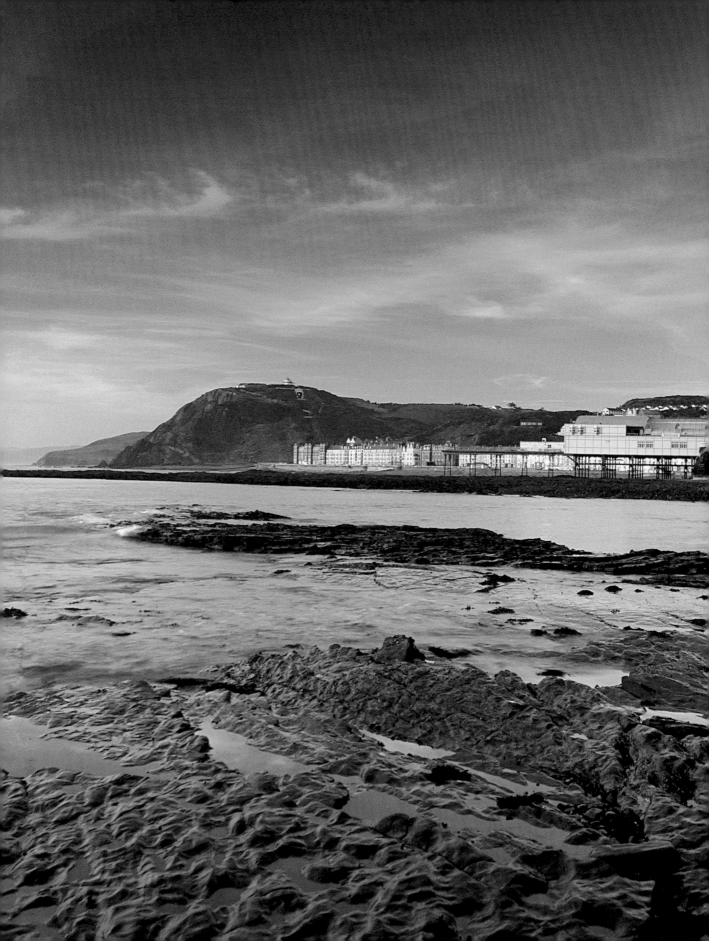

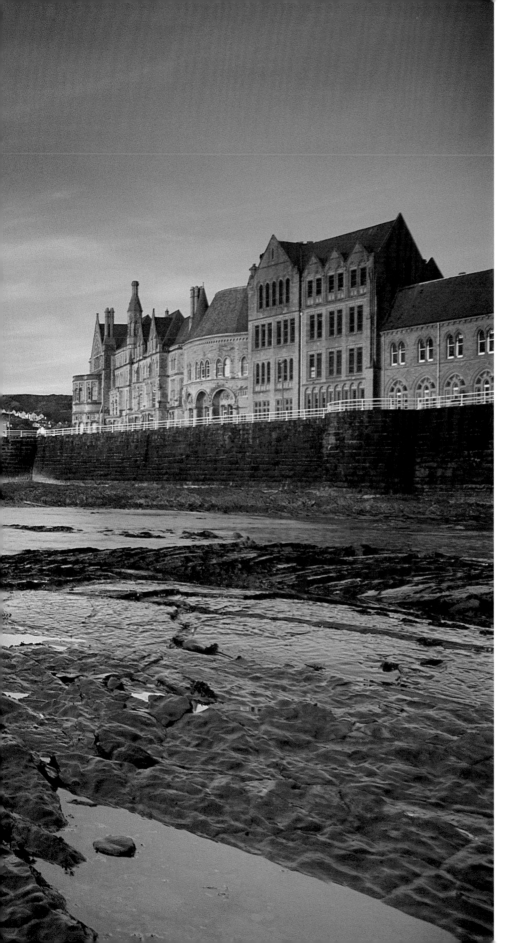

Aberystwyth
With its population swollen during term time, the university town of Aberystwyth – alongside Bangor, Wrexham, Lampeter, Swansea, Cardiff and Newport – engages in a significant Welsh industry, that of learning. Visit the exhibitions of maps and manuscripts at the National Library of Wales, to see how our relationship with the landscape has evolved over many centuries.
Photographer, Dave Newbould.

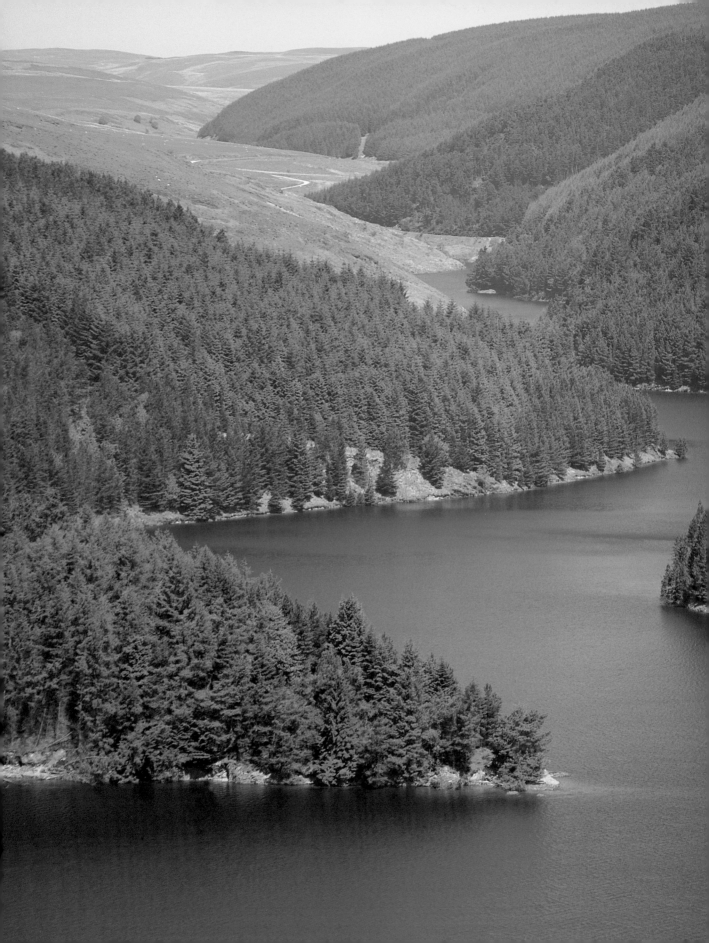

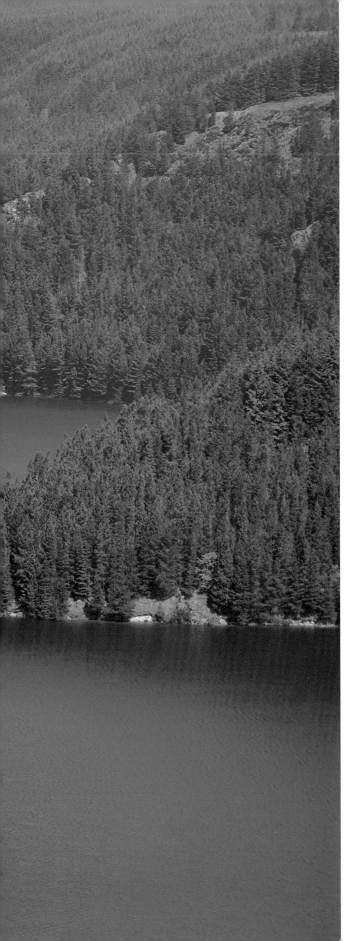

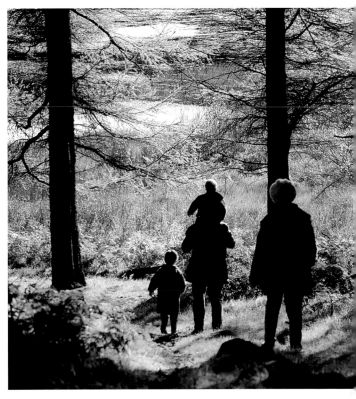

Llyn Brianne
Inland Ceredigion provides
wonderful opportunities
to unwind in spacious
countryside. In times gone
by, the inhabitants of these
hills used to make their way
every Sunday, on foot or on
horseback, to the remote
chapel of Soar y Mynydd,
where services are still
occasionally held. Learn why
the Romans built a road
through this part of Wales
at the Dolau Cothi gold
mines, near Lampeter,
and see Welsh gold being
worked into Celtic designs
at the Welsh Gold Centre,
Tregaron.
Photographer, Neil Turner.

Bwlch Nant yr Arian
The Forest Visitor Centre at
Bwlch Nant yr Arian, near
Ponterwyd, is a good place
to learn about wildlife and
to watch Red Kites, which
are fed here daily. Two
waymarked walks, beginning
at the visitor centre, give
views of the Rheidol and
Melindwr valleys – and of
Plynlimon, the highest
mountain in mid Wales.
Photographer, Jeremy Moore.

Brecon Beacons

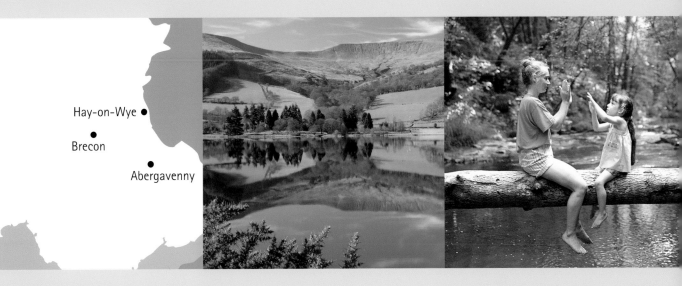

Hay-on-Wye ●

● Brecon

● Abergavenny

The distinctive summits of the Brecon Beacons tower over the valleys and pasturelands of Wales's second-largest national park. This landscape of rock, moorland, rivers and waterfalls is within easy reach of Cardiff and Swansea.

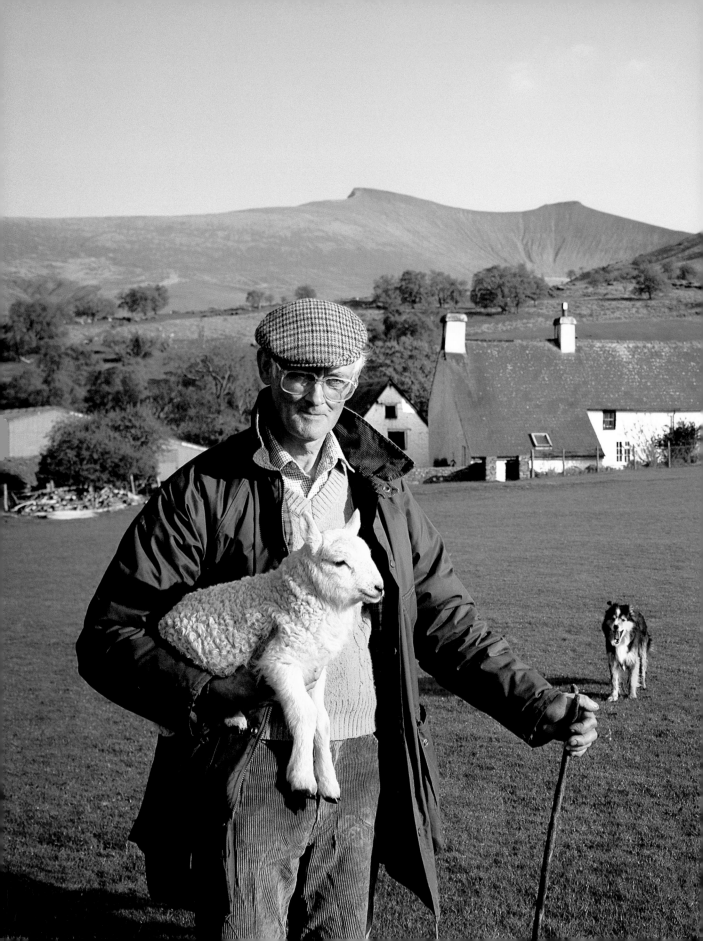

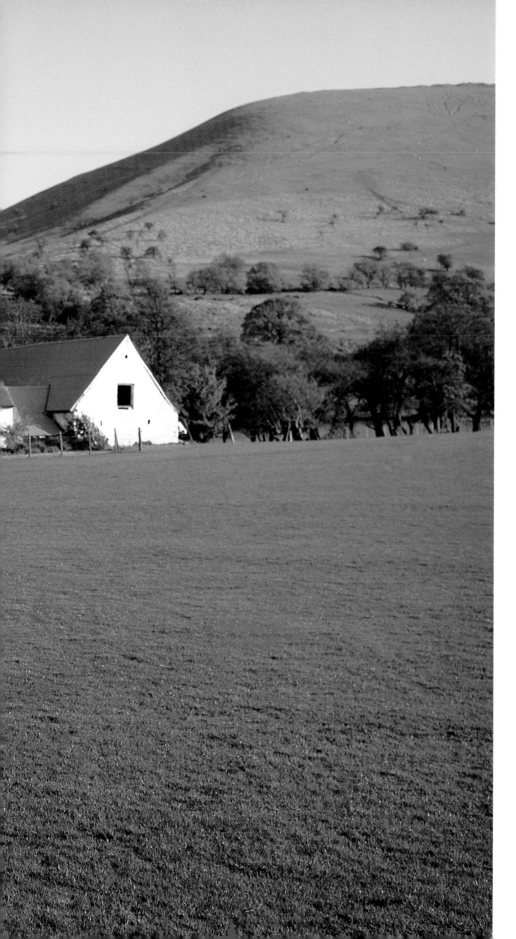

Upland Farm
Farming has shaped this land since mankind progressed from being a hunter-gatherer to keeping animals and growing crops. Local produce includes Welsh beef and lamb, salmon, game, honey, cider, cheese and pure, crystal-clear water piped from far underground. Taste and buy good food at the farmers' market held in Brecon each month – or visit the Royal Welsh Agricultural Show in Builth Wells during July. Photographer, Harry Williams.

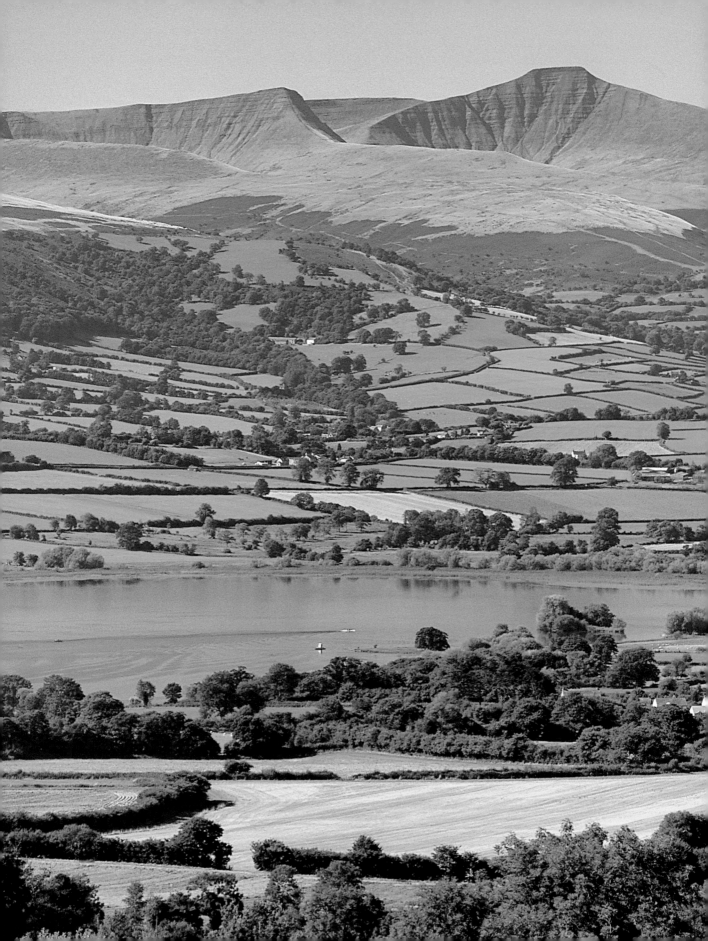

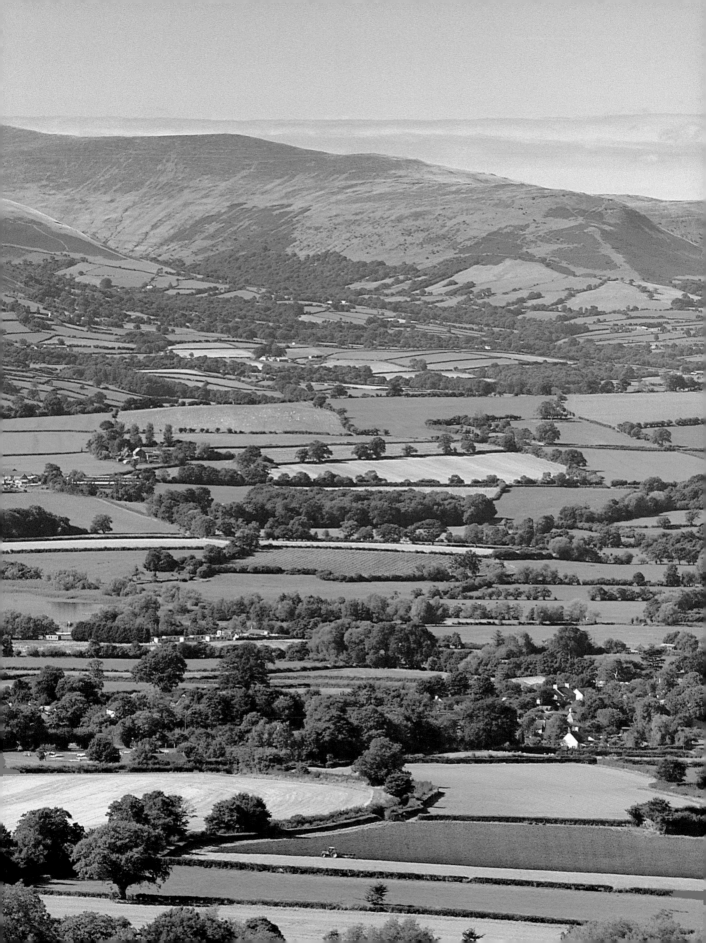

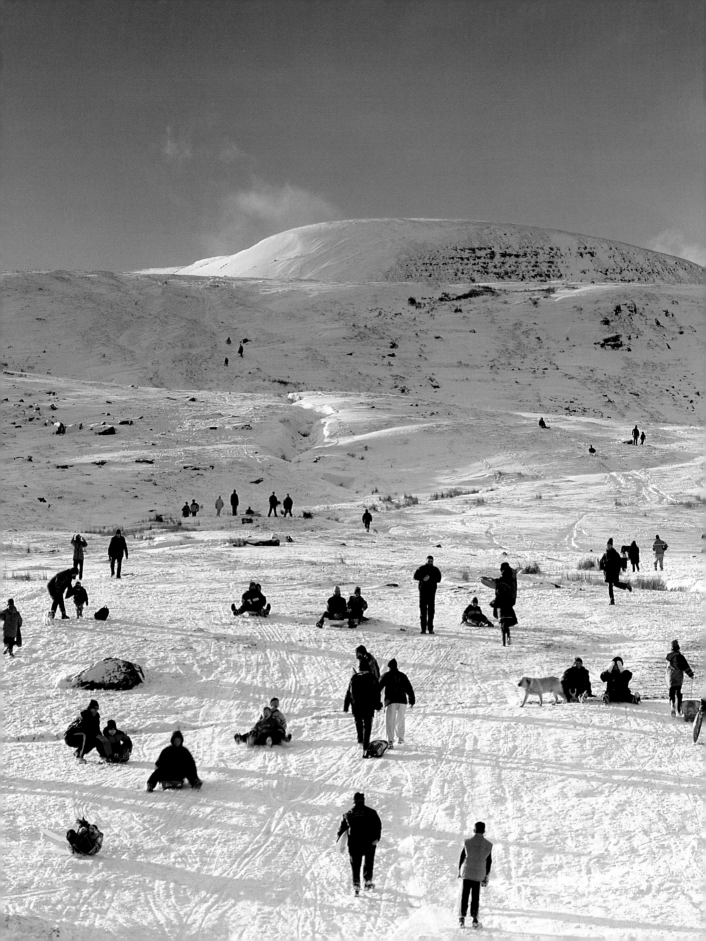

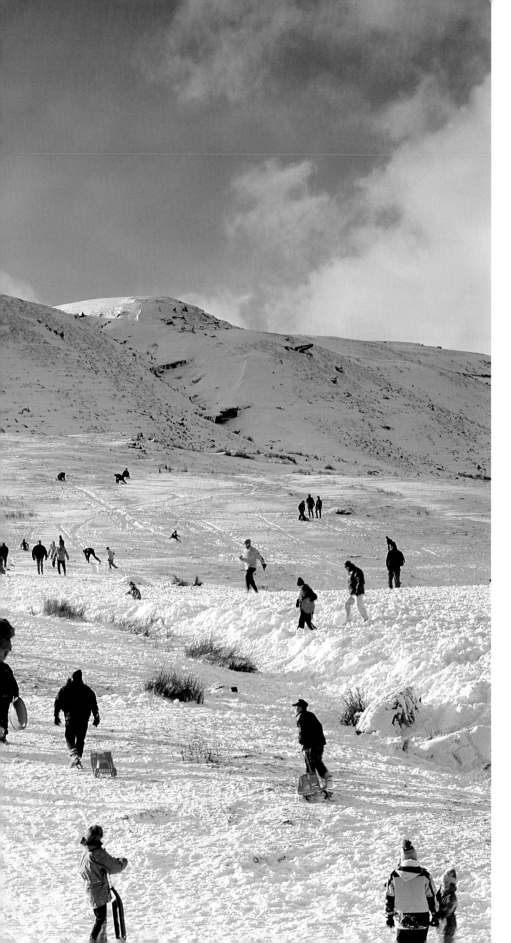

Llangorse Lake Pages 106/107
Water-based activities in the park include sailing and windsurfing on Llangorse Lake, cruising the Monmouth and Brecon Canal, and reservoir fishing at several locations. Enjoy a relaxing walk around Llangorse Lake, from the car park near the sailing club – the bird life is especially rich in the reed beds and water meadows.
Photographer, Jeremy Moore.

Sledging
Winter is a great time to visit – not only for committed mountaineers, but for families keen to enjoy accessible sledging without having to trek too far from the car parks. The A470, the main north-south road through Wales, traverses the national park and is usually kept clear even when the mountains are glistening under fresh snow.
Photographer, Billy Stock.

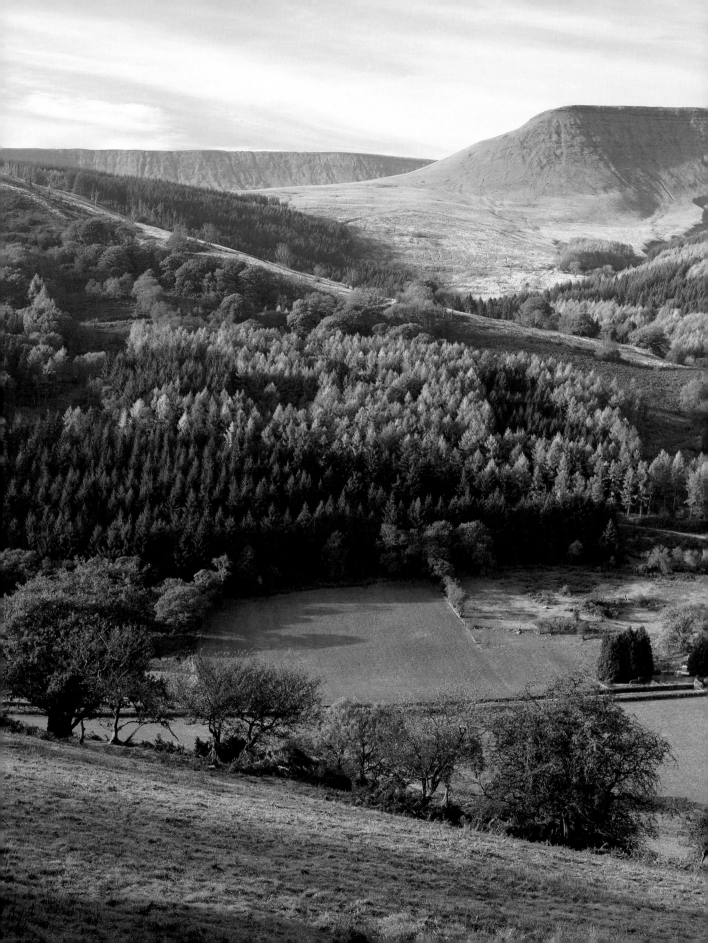

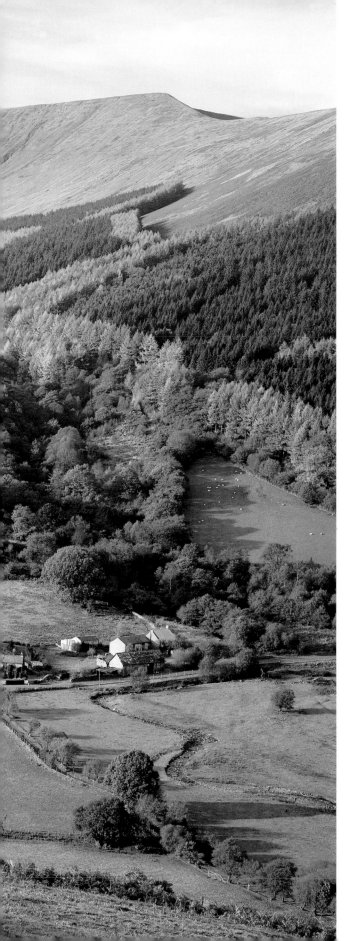

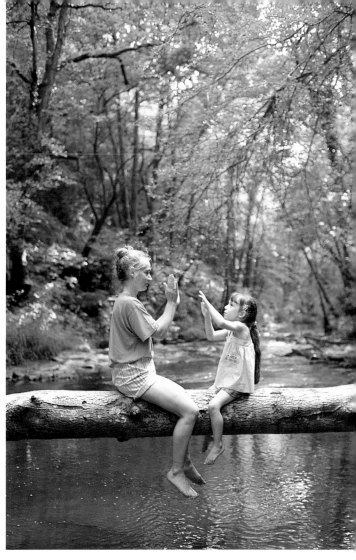

Waun Rydd
Walking, climbing and pot-holing are popular in the Brecon Beacons, and the intimidating hills and boggy moorlands have a well-deserved reputation as the toughest of military training areas. Call at the Brecon Beacons visitor centre, near Libanus, for details outdoor activities.
Photographer, Graham Morley.

Family friendly
Less strenuous options include the Brecon Mountain Railway, the Dan yr Ogof caves, pony trekking or communing with nature in any of a thousand magical spots. Get your bearings in the visitor centre at Craig y Nos Country Park in the upper Swansea Valley, in surroundings that were home to 19th-century opera star Adelina Patti.
Photographer, Steve Benbow.

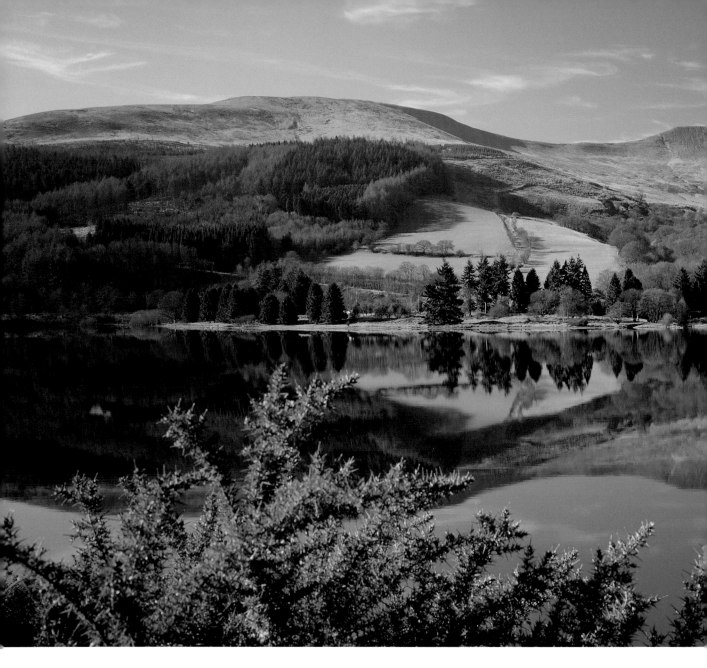

Talybont Reservoir
The changing seasons reward repeated visits – to experience fresh spring foliage, the lushness of summer and that first chill hint of autumn when, from the high ridges, you can see fifty miles in the clear air. From the A40 east of Brecon, take the B4558 for views of the Brecon Beacons and Usk Valley from Llanfrynach, Talybont-on-Usk and Crickhowell. Be sure to see, but take care crossing, the extremely narrow packhorse bridge over the Usk at Llangynidr. Photographer, Graham Morley.

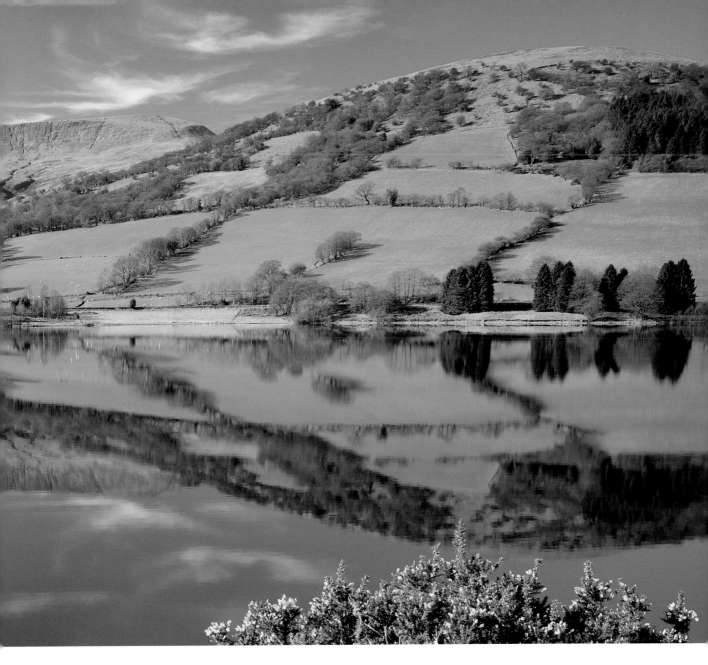

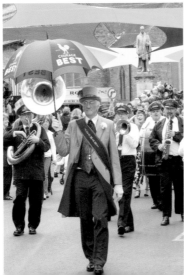

Brecon Jazz Festival
Held each August, this major festival sees Brecon pulsating to the sound of jazz. The region also has country shows, food festivals, sheepdog trials and horse fairs – details from tourist information centres. Photographer, Brian Woods.

Historic Borderlands

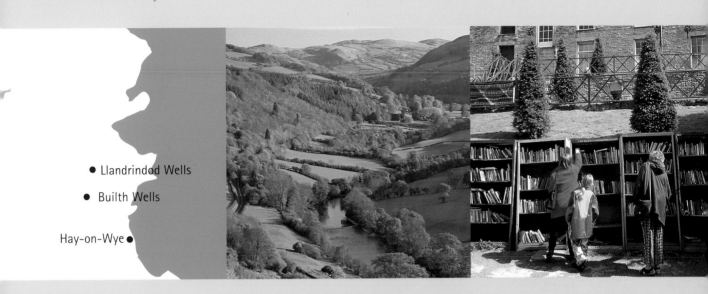

Llandrindod Wells

Builth Wells

Hay-on-Wye

Wales is bounded by the sea on three sides and by a change in terrain from upland to lowland along the fourth. The border with England was set by the Saxon King Offa of Mercia in the 8th century and has remained much the same ever since.

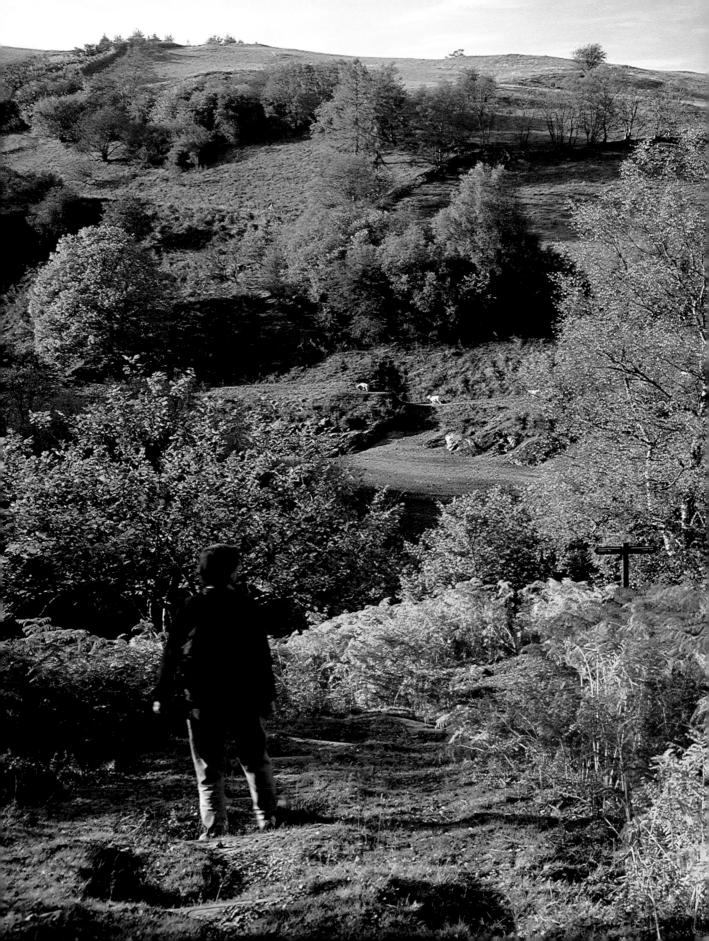

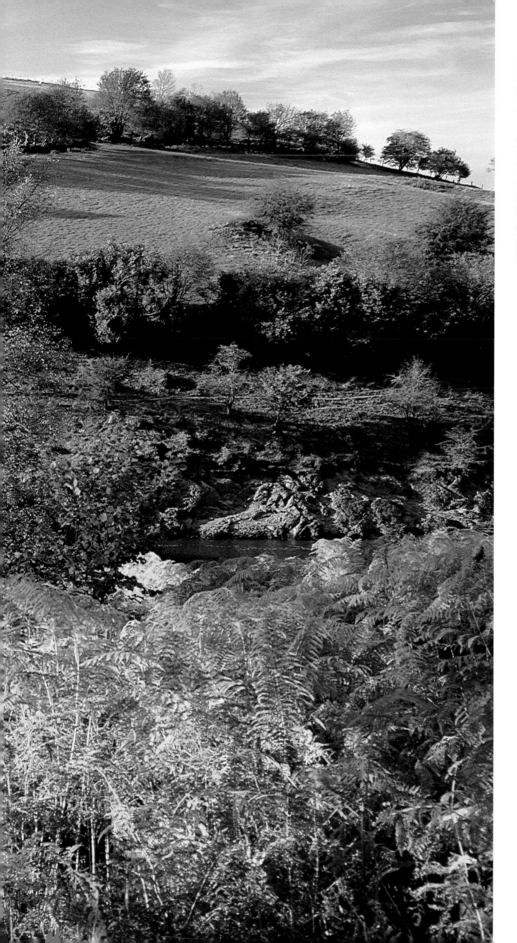

Glyndŵr Way
Charismatic leader Owain Glyndŵr united much of Wales between 1400 and 1410. A long-distance footpath links Machynlleth, where he held his parliament, and Sycharth – near Welshpool – where he came to prominence as a landowning chieftain. Pick up a trail leaflet and walk part of the Glyndŵr Way. Photographer, Jeremy Moore.

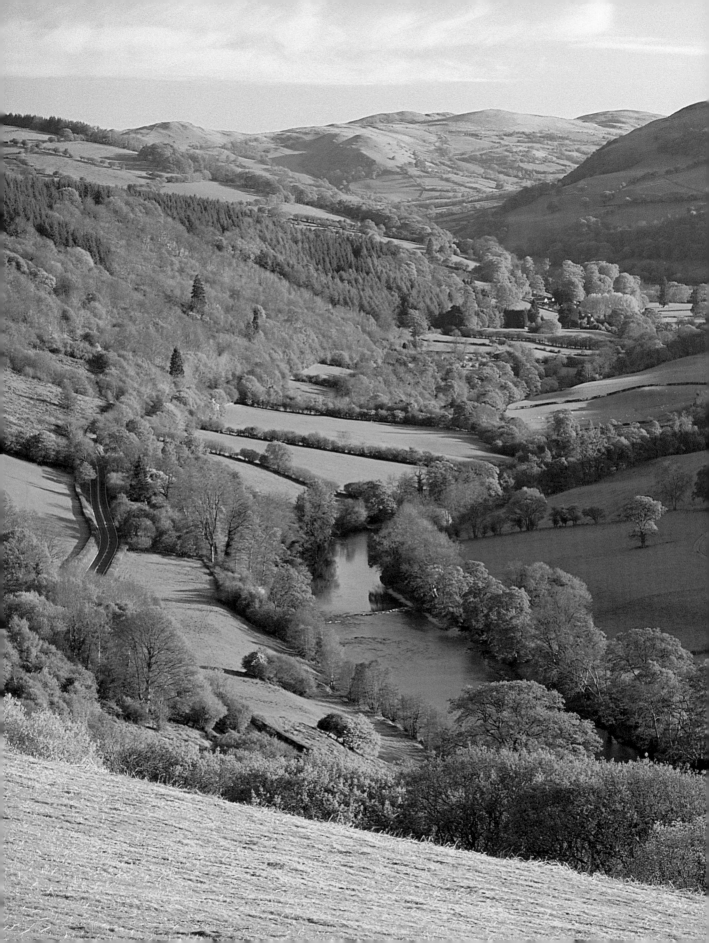

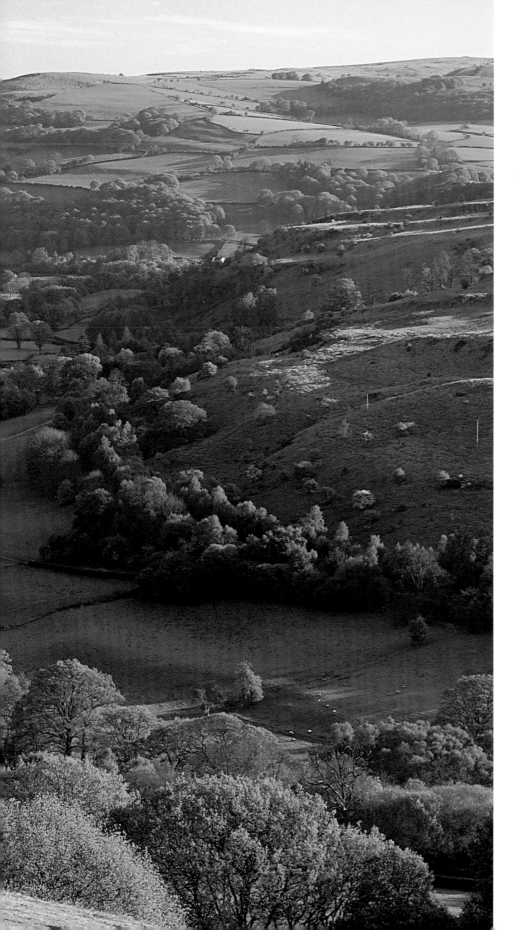

River Wye
Far from their origins on
Plynlimon Fawr, the Severn
and Wye, our longest rivers,
meander through Powys then
head off into England for a
while – before eventually
finding the sea at the south-
eastern corner of Wales.
Visit any of the attractive river
towns – Newtown, Welshpool,
Monmouth or Chepstow –
to sense their importance as
commercial and administrative
centres for the rural hinterland.
Photographer, Jeremy Moore.

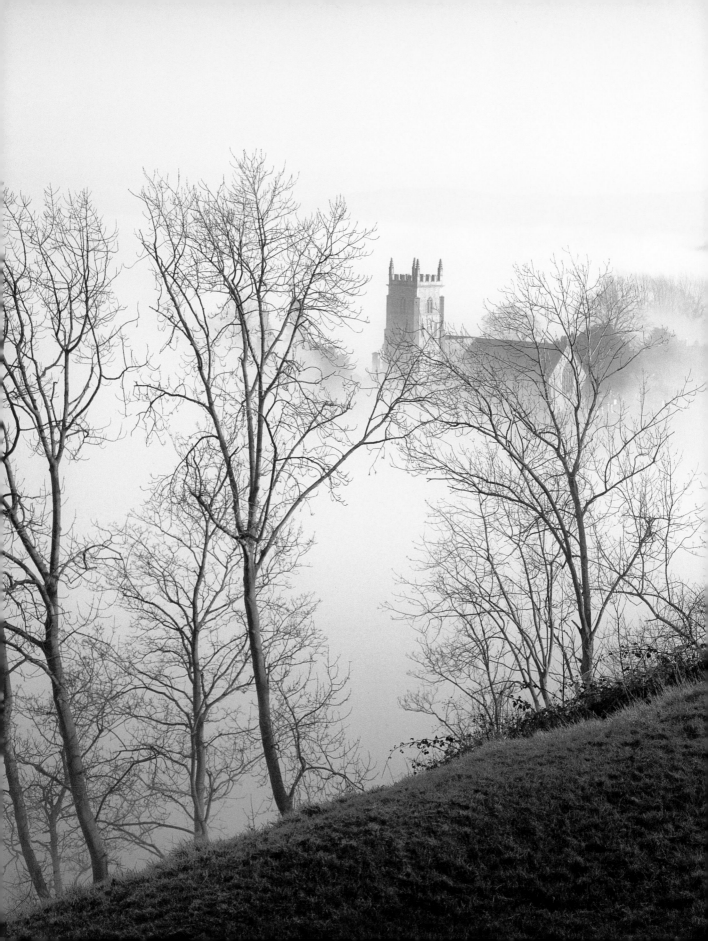

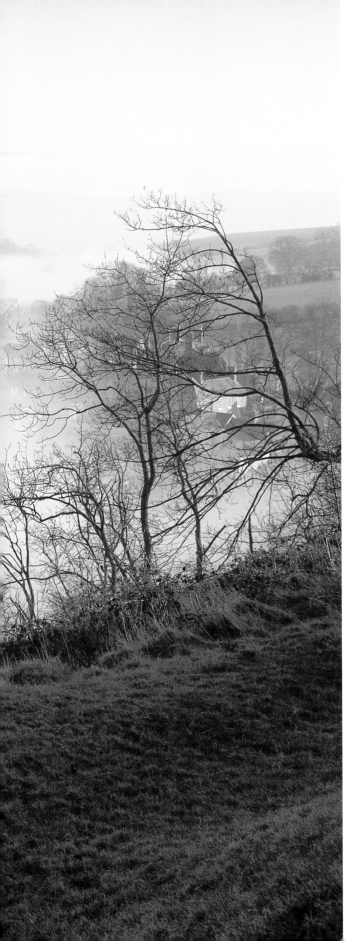

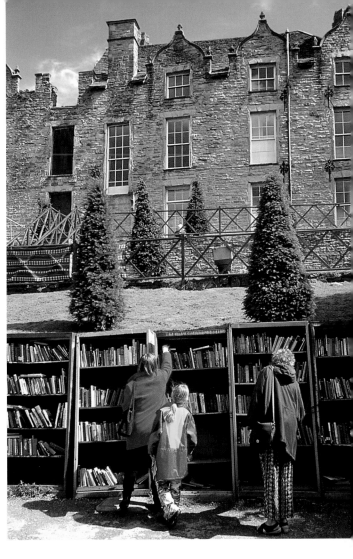

Montgomery
The miniature towns of Montgomery, Knighton and Presteigne have changed little since the squire and the parson trod their narrow streets and quaint squares. Walk up to Montgomery's elevated castle, for wide views over the town and countryside – or visit the Offa's Dyke centre in Knighton and tackle a section of the long-distance path.
Photographers,
Janet and Colin Bord.

Hay Festival of Literature
Hay-on-Wye, the town of books, hosts its prestigious literary gathering in May, and has the world's highest concentration of bookstores. Join the authors, bookworms and glitterati who congregate at the festival – or call by at any time to visit the bookshops and excellent craft centre.
Photographer, David Williams.

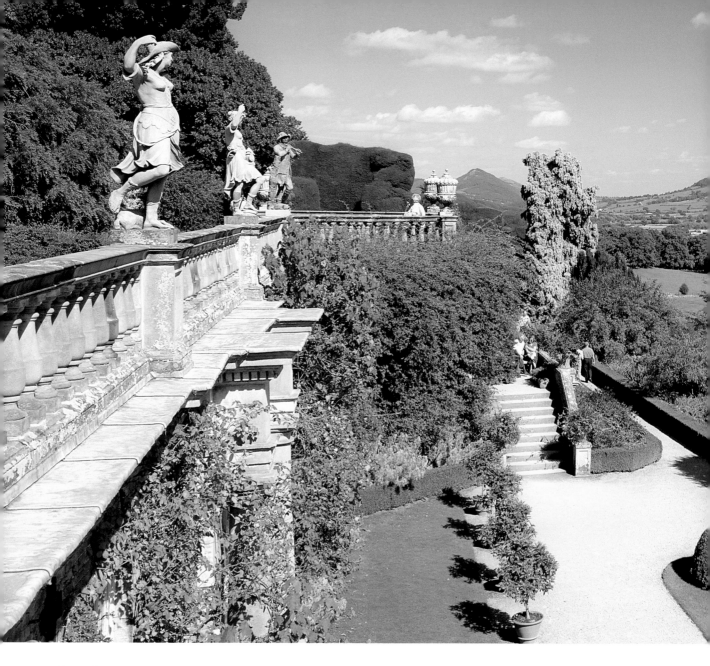

Powis Castle
The formal terraces and sculpted gardens of Powis Castle, near Welshpool, are of the highest horticultural and historical importance. The medieval castle perched above them has some of the finest paintings and furniture in Wales, including treasures brought back by Clive of India. Visit this outstanding National Trust property between April and November – details of opening times and special events from tourist information centres or the trust's website.
Photographer, Chris Warren.

Powis Castle
Grapes are grown at several locations in Wales, and made into award-winning wines. It is said that the Romans brought over the first vines, and planted them on south-facing slopes. At food festivals, agricultural shows and specialist shops, be sure to seek out Welsh wines and spirits – and the honey mead that once fortified Celtic warriors.
Photographer, John Kinsey.

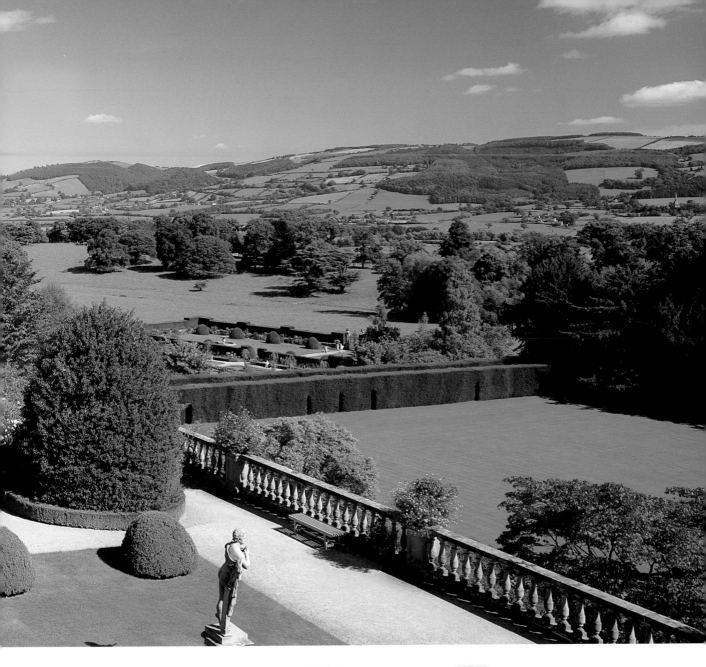

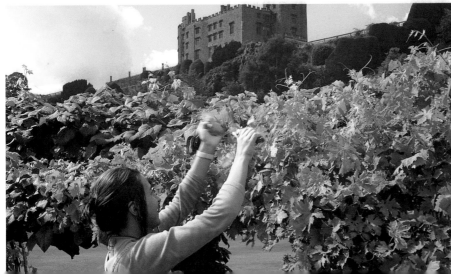

Black Mountains

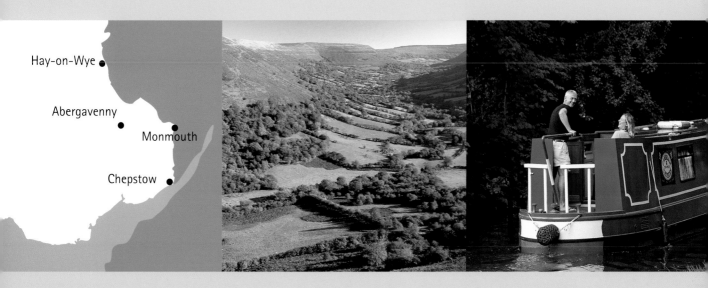

The Black Mountains are a distinct range of rounded hills and ridges in the eastern part of the Brecon Beacons National Park. Sheltered valleys of unexpected remoteness and tranquillity contrast with the heathland above.

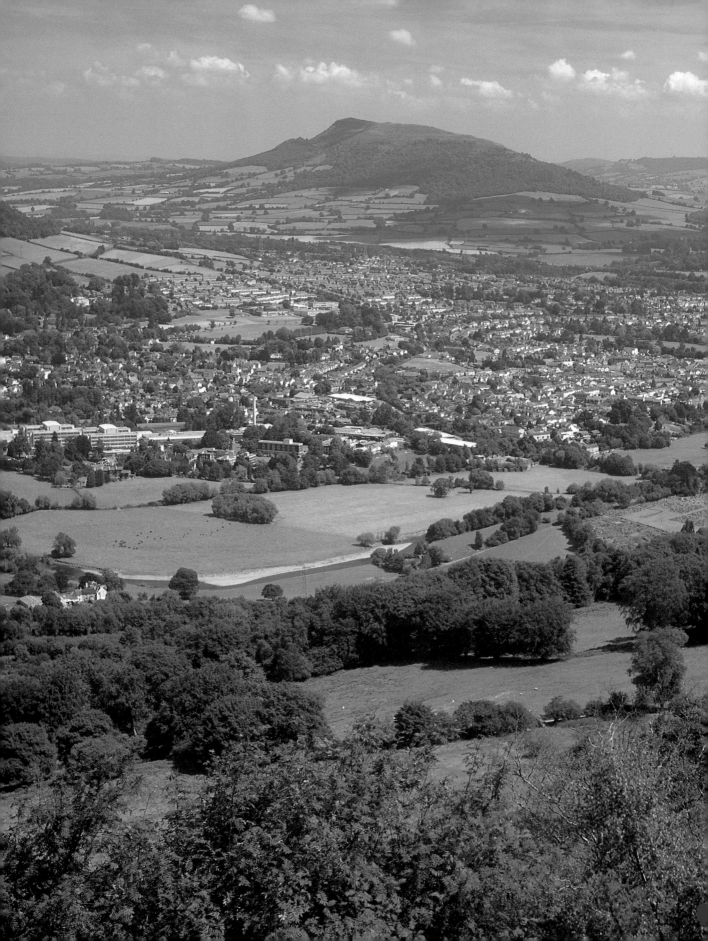

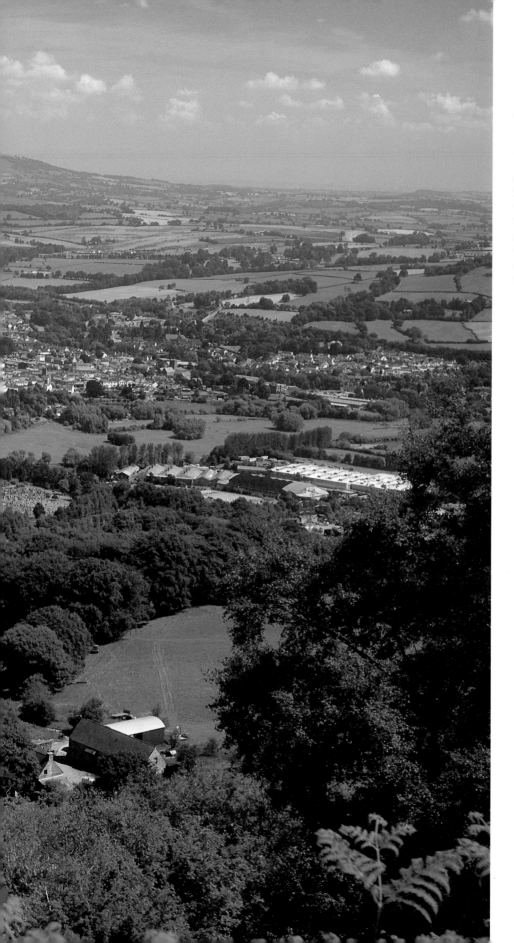

Abergavenny
Skilled producers have made Abergavenny famous as a centre of excellence for food. Top-quality produce is displayed to sumptuous effect at the large covered market, and in numerous independent shops. Visit Abergavenny in September for the food festival – or at any time of year for the specialised food shops and gourmet restaurants that characterise this region of discerning tastes.
Photographer, Graham Morley.

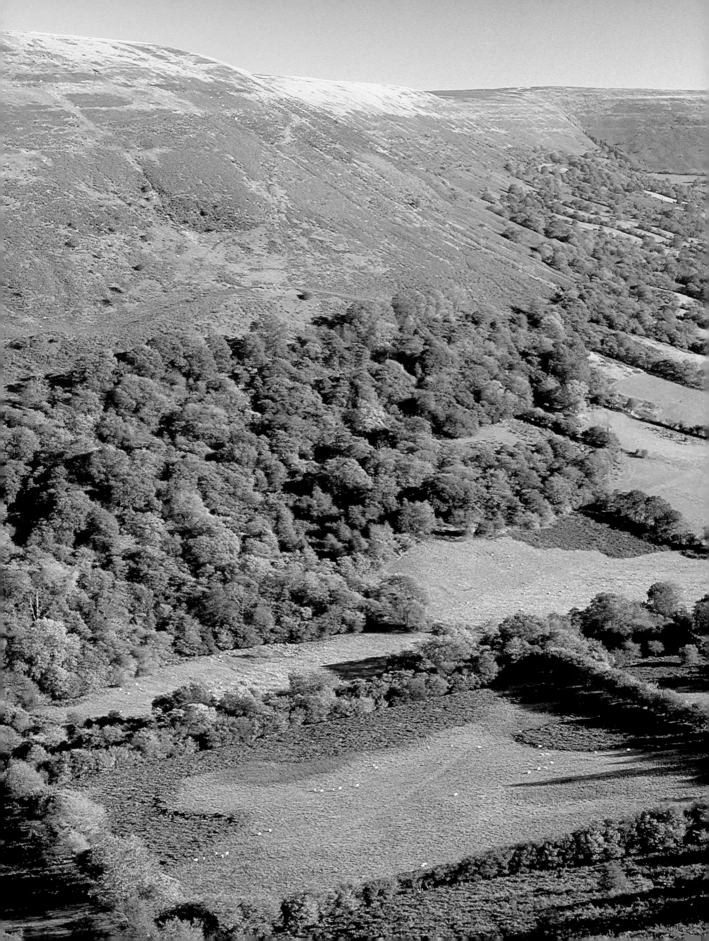

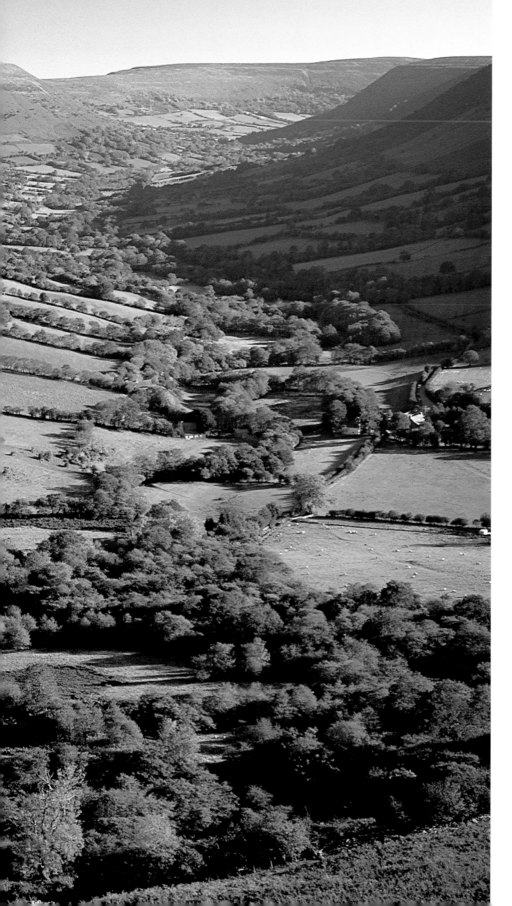

Vale of Ewyas

The Black Mountains, although a serious challenge for walkers, are less barren than the central Brecon Beacons. The Vale of Ewyas – on their eastern edge, bordering England – is a hidden gem. From Llanvihangel Crucorney, take a minor road to Llanthony Priory and continue along a narrow and steepening lane past Capel-y-ffin and over the spectacular Gospel Pass to Hay-on-Wye – it's best to avoid busy weekends. Photographer, Jeremy Moore.

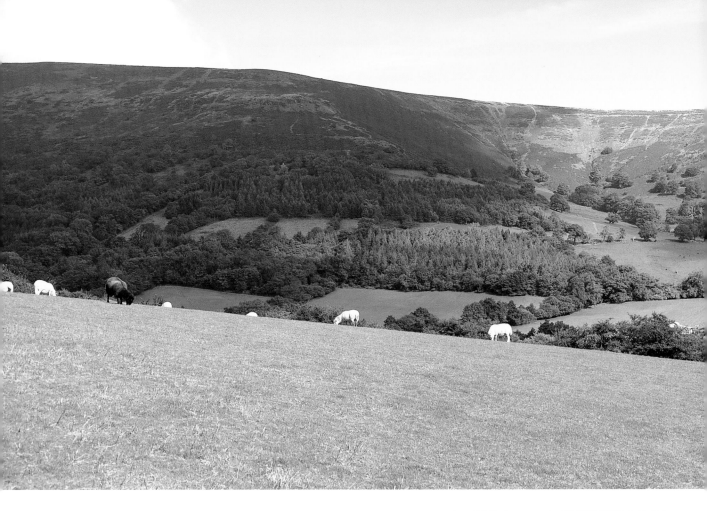

Llanthony Priory

Hidden away in the Vale of Ewyas, Llanthony Priory is a place of such pervading sanctity that medieval traveller Giraldus Cambrensis felt moved to state that nowhere is 'more truly calculated for religion'. A network of marked footpaths radiates from Llanthony Priory – the energetic might like to climb to the summit of Bal Mawr (1,990 ft) for fine views of the neighbouring Grwyne Fawr valley.
Photographer, Harry Williams.

Monmouth and Brecon Canal

A marvellous means of transport to find in a national park, this scenic canal once served the coal and iron industries. Canal cruisers are available for hire, while towpaths provide level walks and cycle rides – details from Goytre Wharf tourist information centre at Llanover, near Abergavenny.
Photographer, John Kinsey.

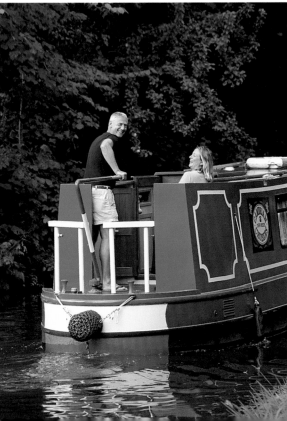

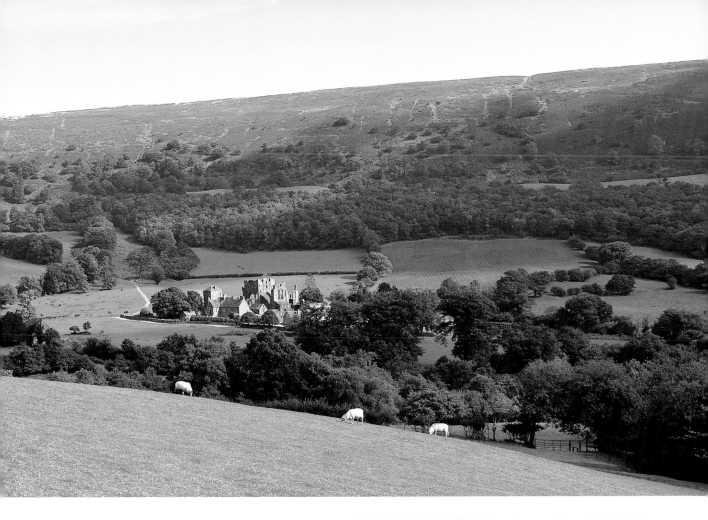

Food for the soul

The Skirrid Inn, said to be one of the oldest in Wales, and the legendary Walnut Tree restaurant are just two of many places hereabouts where good food and great atmosphere combine.

The Taste of Wales scheme promotes excellence in the preparation and presentation of Welsh produce – look for the logo that identifies members.

Photographer, Neil Turner.

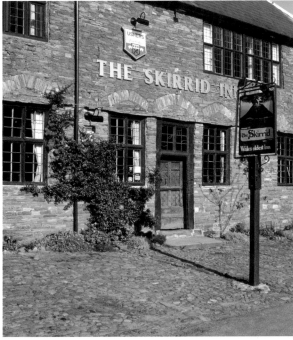

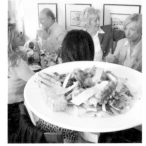

Photographer, Jeff Morgan.

The Valleys

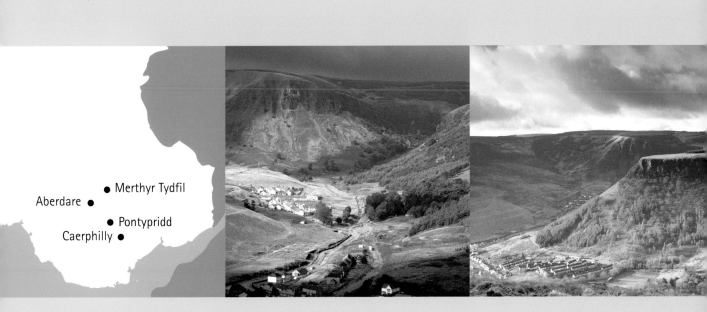

Aberdare ●

● Merthyr Tydfil

● Pontypridd

Caerphilly ●

From the mid-19th century onward, a thousand square miles south of the Brecon Beacons became transformed by coal mining. These valleys have been made green once more by a massive government land reclamation programme, with new leisure centres, schools, housing, business and industry parks.

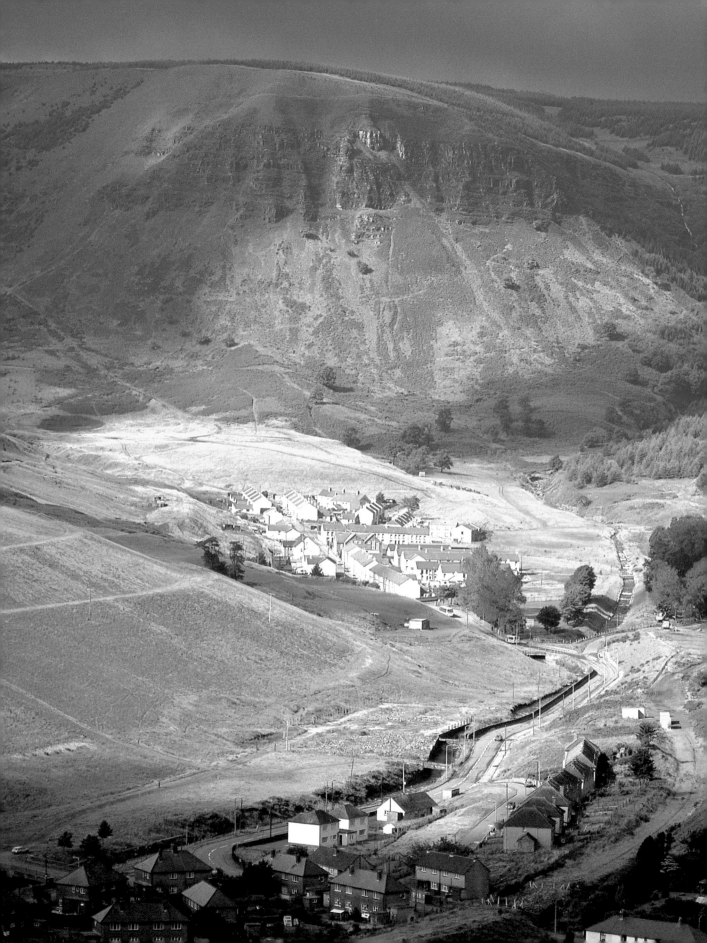

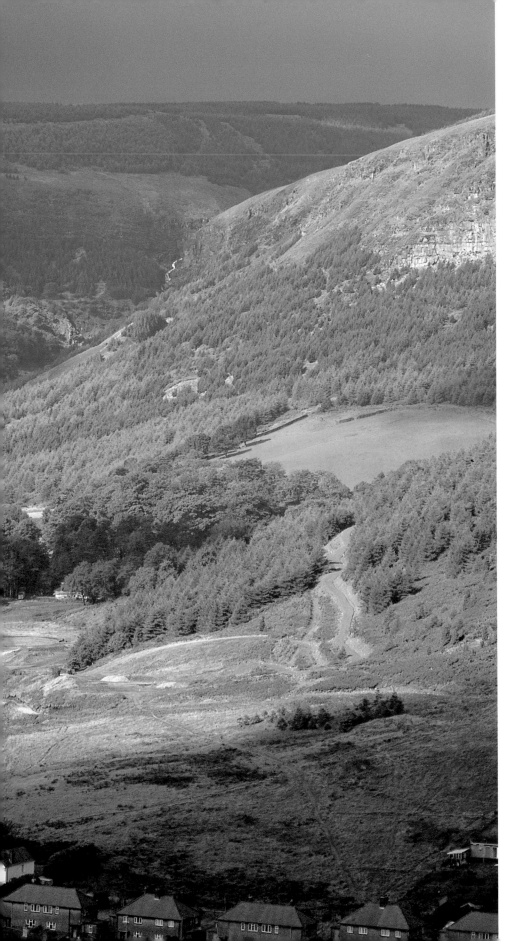

Blaen–cwm, Rhondda Fawr
After 150 years of intense activity – Wales once supplied a third of the world's coal – these archetypal mining valleys are becoming green again. The only mine to survive the disappearance of the industry in recent decades, Tower Colliery, is beyond the ridge in the distance. Drive up the Rhondda Fawr valley from Pontypridd (A4058/4061) to the ridge above Hirwaun and Tower Colliery, then back down the Rhondda Fach from Aberdare (A4233) – through legendary mining towns including Treorchy, Treherbert, Maerdy, Ferndale and Llwynypia.
Photographer, Neil Turner.

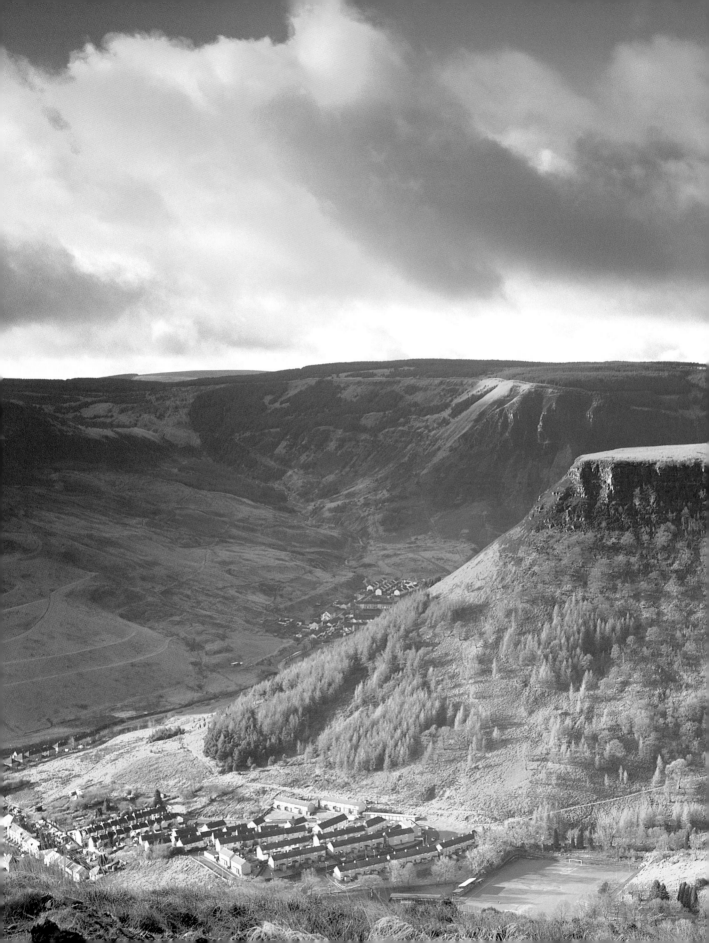

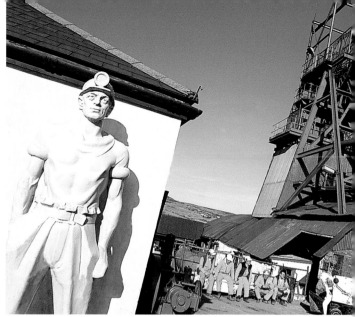

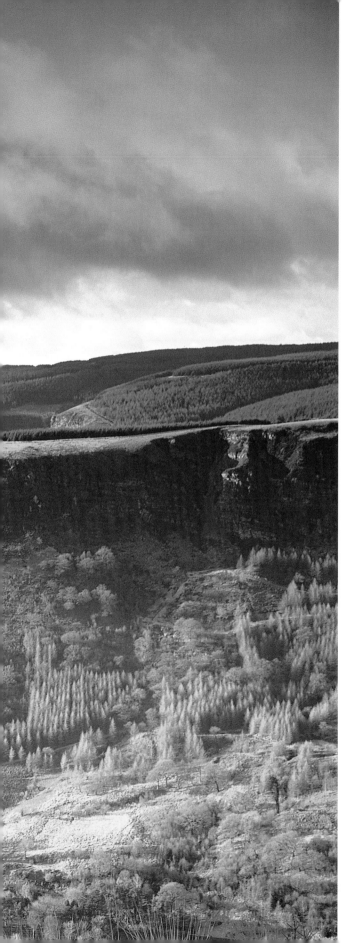

Rhondda Valley

With their closely packed terraced houses, chapels and miners' institutes, the valley towns were a ferment of life and culture. The early 1900s saw a quarter of a million men working underground. Visit the great houses built by the coal and iron barons – the Marquis of Bute's incredible Gothic Revival fantasy at Cardiff Castle, and William Crawshay's solid Cyfarthfa Castle at Merthyr Tydfil.
Photographer, Derek Rees.

Blaenavon

The hills around Blaenavon's Big Pit mining museum provided all the ingredients for iron making – iron ore, coal and limestone. There, and at the Rhondda Heritage Park near Pontypridd, the pithead winding gear stands as a monument to those who risked their lives below. The Blaenavon Industrial Landscape is a UNESCO World Heritage Site – join a former miner for an underground tour of Big Pit and visit the ironworks, built in 1788, which supplied the Industrial Revolution.
Photographer, Ken Dickinson.

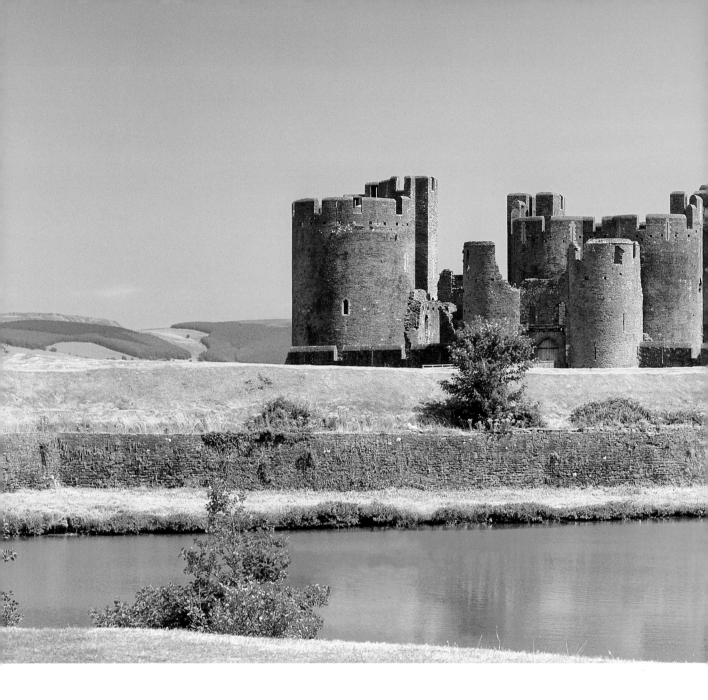

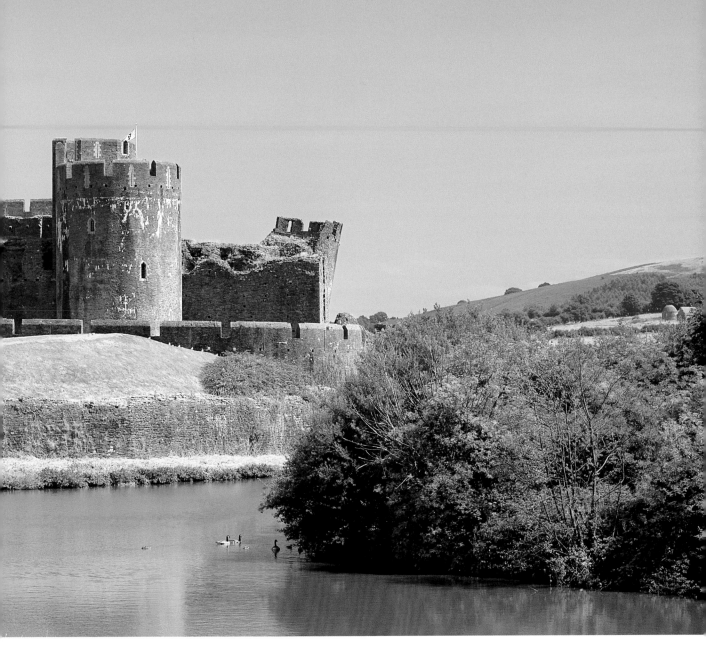

Caerphilly Castle
Built by Gilbert de Clare
in the late 13th century,
Caerphilly Castle is an
excellent example of walls-
within-walls defences.
This splendidly moated
fortress, the largest in Wales,
has a fine banqueting hall
and a tower that leans more
than that of Pisa.

Try to catch one of the
battle re-enactment days,
when armour glints, swords
clash and replicas of Roman
catapults and medieval siege
engines are demonstrated.
Photographer, Chris Warren.

Teifi Valley and inland Pembrokeshire

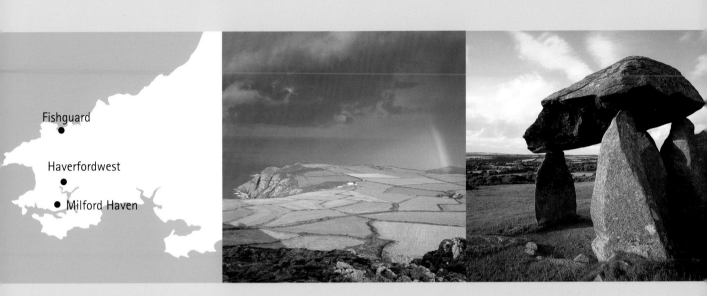

The River Teifi flows along a valley of great beauty from the Teifi Pools, near Strata Florida Abbey, to the sea at Aberteifi – Cardigan. For much of its length, it forms a natural boundary between Ceredigion and Pembrokeshire.

Fishguard

Haverfordwest

Milford Haven

Preseli Hills
Modest in altitude but full of mystery, the Preseli Hills of Pembrokeshire are said to hide the gateway to the Celtic underworld, Annwn, and to have provided the bluestone megaliths for Stonehenge. Visit the reconstructed Iron Age settlement at Castell Henllys, to learn about our Celtic ancestors.
Photographer, Aled Hughes.

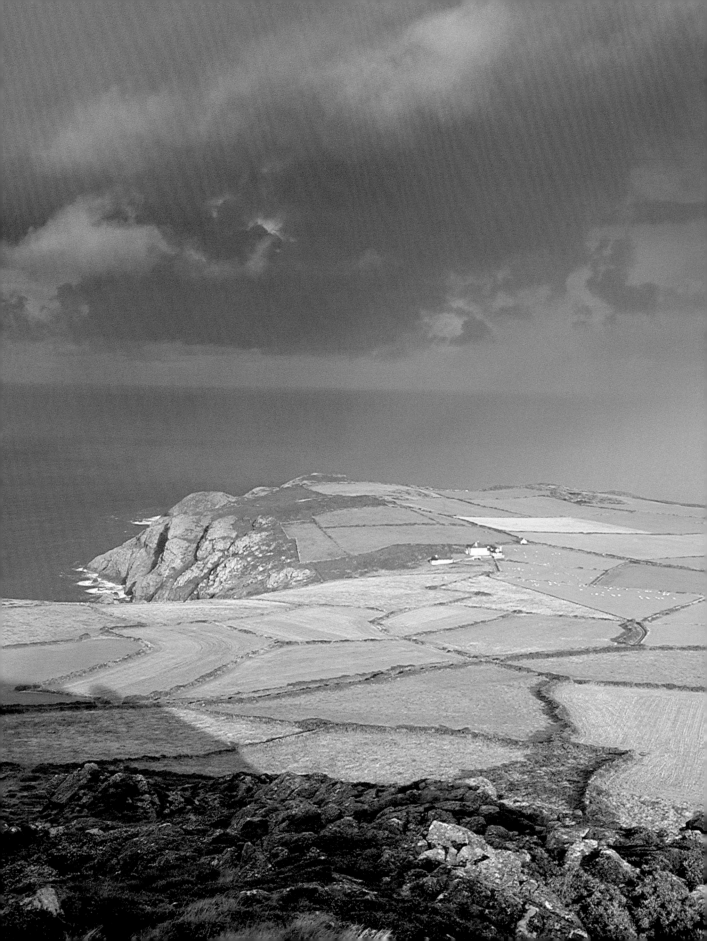

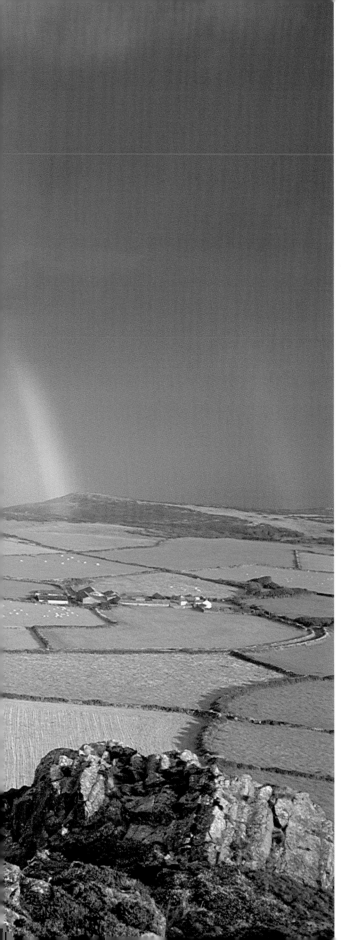

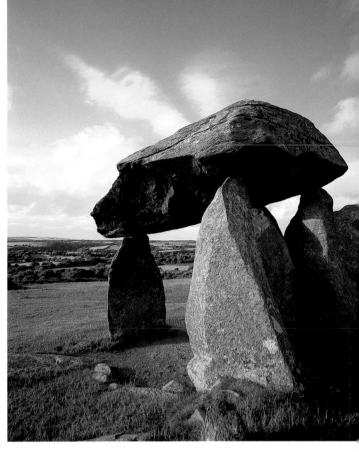

Pembrokeshire farmland
Much of northern
Pembrokeshire is covered by
an intricate pattern of small
fields dovetailed between
rocks and hard places. In the
Gwaun Valley, the old Julian
calendar is still used –
giving a great excuse to
extend the New Year
celebrations by a couple
of weeks. From Fishguard,
feel time seemingly running
backwards as you follow
the valley of the river
Gwaun inland, through the
Preseli Hills.
Photographer, Jeremy Moore.

Pentre Ifan
Pembrokeshire has many
Neolithic sites – the sea
was both a food source
and a highway for the
early inhabitants of Wales.
The capstone of the Pentre
Ifan burial chamber,
supported on pointed stone
pillars, is around 13ft long.
Seek out the cromlechs
(stone monuments) at Pentre
Ifan and Carreg Sampson,
near Abercastle, built some
5,000 years ago.
Photographer, Chris Warren.

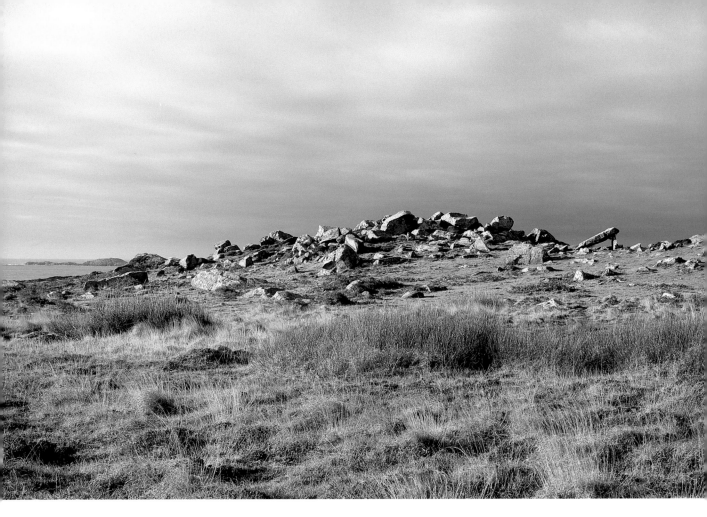

Rocks of Ages

This is an immensely ancient landscape. All the rocks underlying Pembrokeshire date back at least 300 million years, mostly to the Palaeozoic Era – although some pre-Cambrian outcrops are 1,000 million years old. Walk up Garn Fawr near Pwll Deri, or Carn Ingli near Newport, to see remains of Iron Age hill settlements among the jumbled rocks.
Photographer, Aled Hughes.

Cenarth

Primitive coracles – easily carried, one-man wicker craft covered in tarred canvas – are still used, and even raced, on the Teifi. This is one of Wales's best fishing rivers, especially for sewin – sea trout. The old watermill at Cenarth Falls, west of Newcastle Emlyn, contains a museum – with displays explaining traditional fishing methods.
Photographer, Rob Stratton.

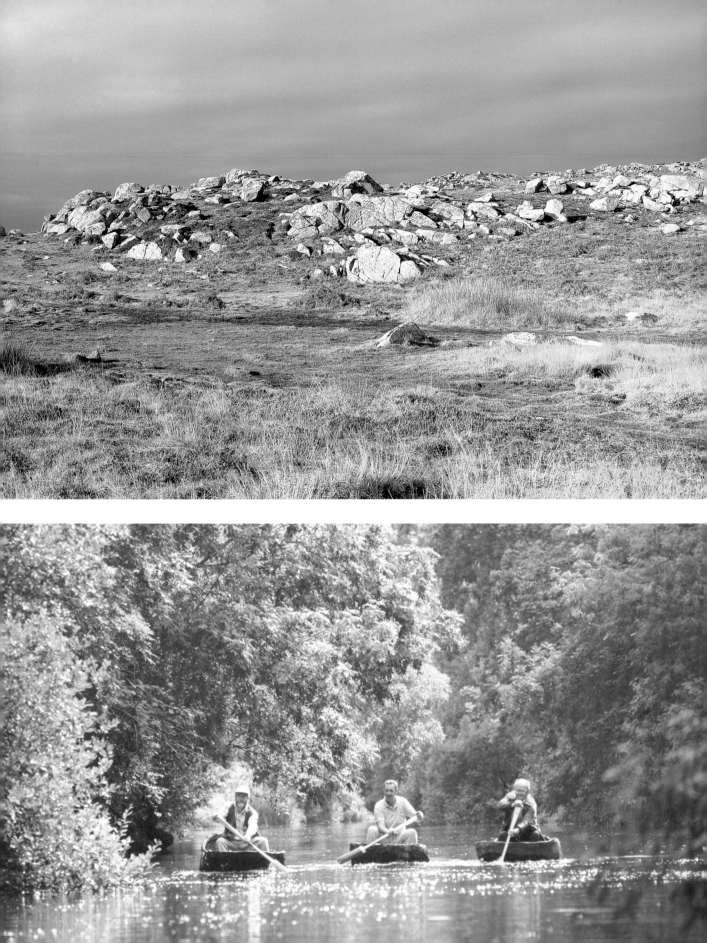

Pembrokeshire Coast

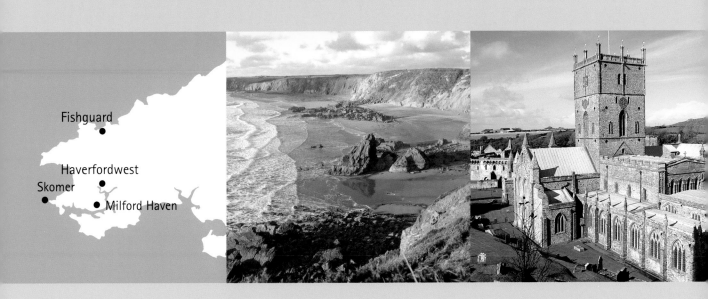

Pembrokeshire has the only coastline in Wales, or England, to be designated a national park on account of its natural history and geological features. The 186-mile Pembrokeshire Coast Path passes picturesque harbours, broad sandy bays, rocky coves and fascinating cliff formations.

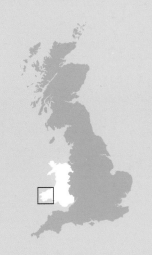

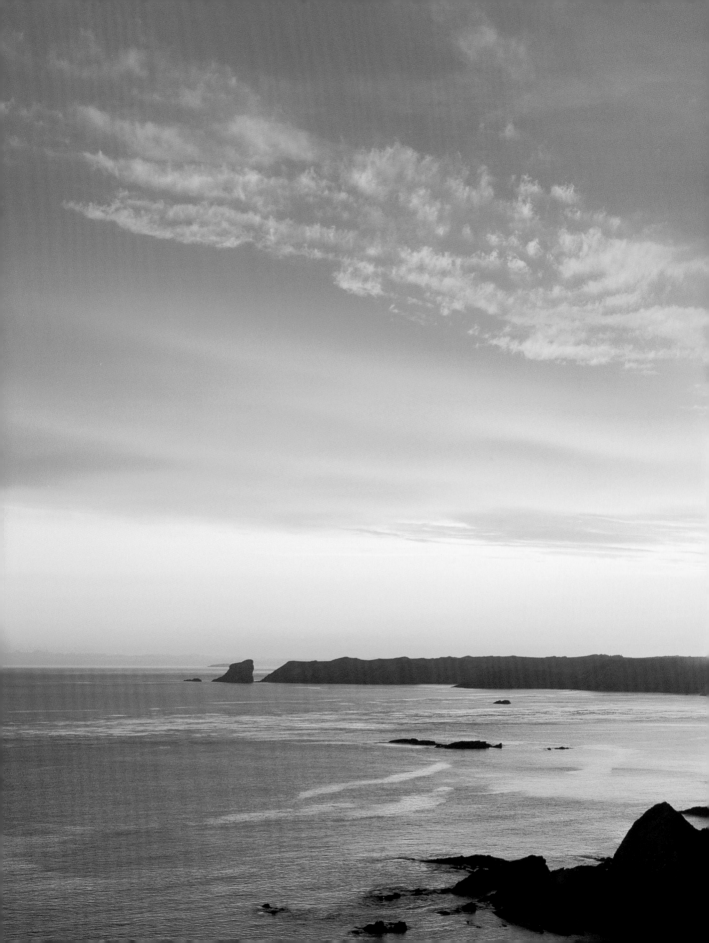

Skomer
The island of Skomer is a nature reserve managed by Wildlife Trust West Wales. It has important populations of seabirds – including Manx shearwater, storm petrel, puffin, guillemot, razorbill and kittiwake – spring and early summer are the best times to see them. Take the seasonal ferry service to Skomer from Martin Haven. Keen bird-watchers stay overnight, to see storm petrels and vast colonies of Manx shearwater at their nesting burrows. Photographer, Andrew Davies.

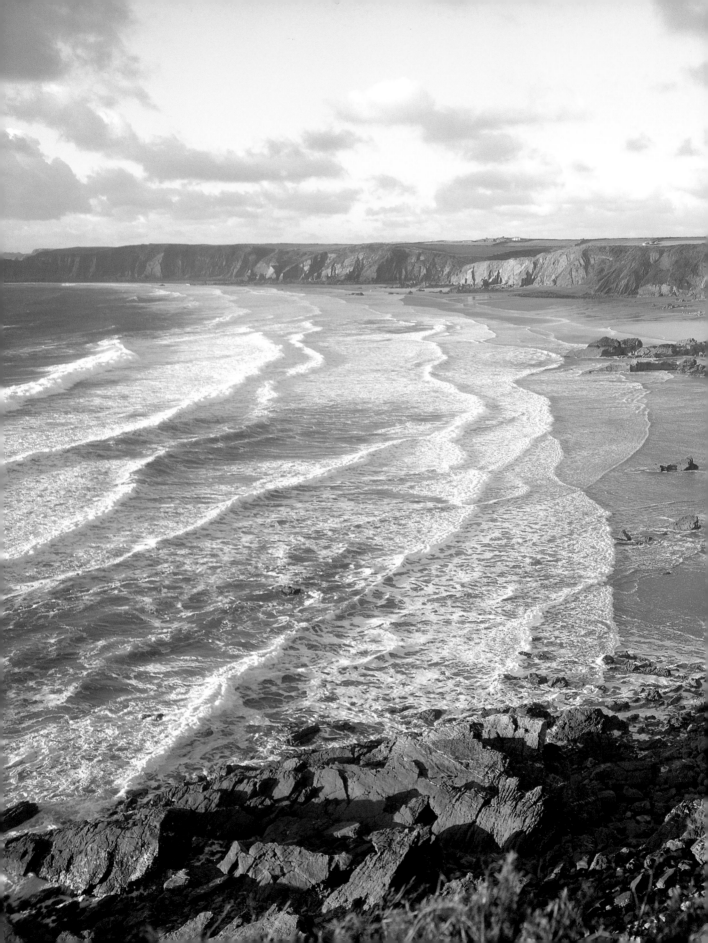

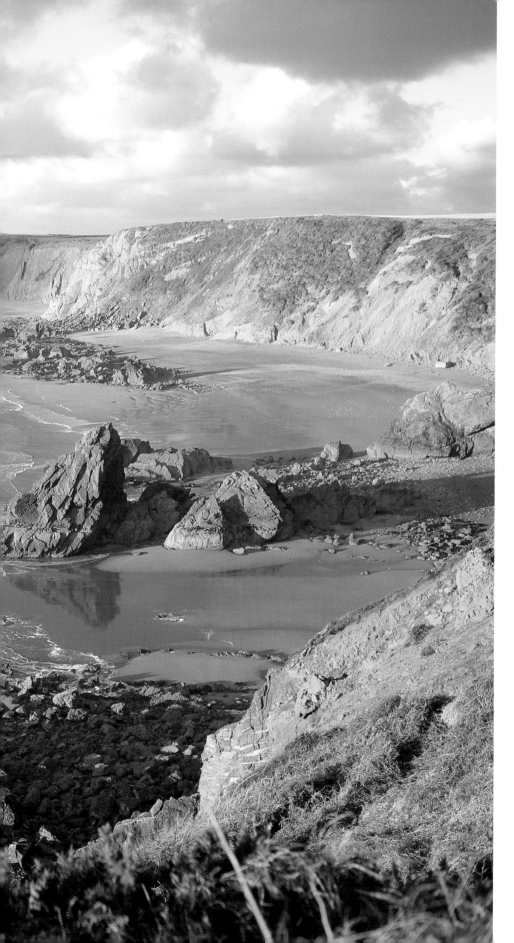

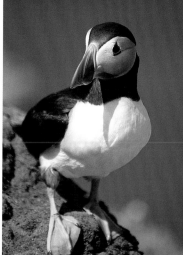

Puffin
These entertaining birds nest in colonies on Skokholm and Skomer from April to July – and spend the rest of the year at sea. Limited access to Skokholm, including overnight stays, is administered by the Wildlife Trust West Wales. Photographer, Andrew Davies.

Marloes Sands
This is one of Pembrokeshire's most beautiful beaches. There are fascinating rock formations at Three Chimneys – where tilted bands of sandstone and mudstone have been eroded at different rates, to great effect. From the National Trust car park at Runwayskiln, follow the coast path south-eastward for some three miles to Great Castle Head and St Ann's Head – or westward a mile or so to Martin Haven. Photographer, Andrew Davies.

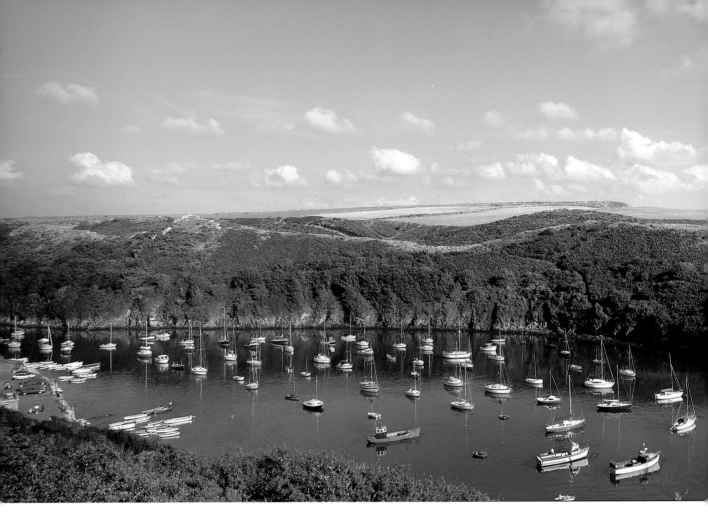

Coasteering

This exciting activity involves swimming, scrambling and climbing along a stretch of coastline in wet suits, buoyancy aids and protective helmets – under the supervision of a qualified instructor. Pembrokeshire offers just about every aquatic sport – ask at one of the numerous harbourside or beachfront centres. Photographer, Andrew Davies.

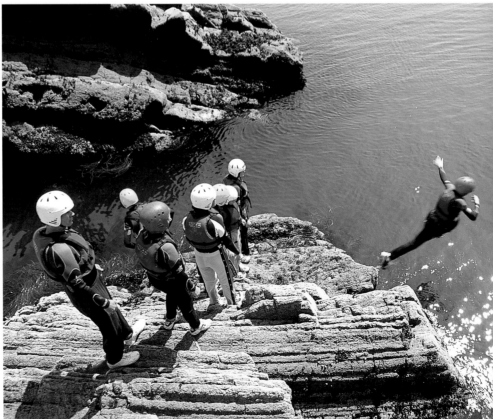

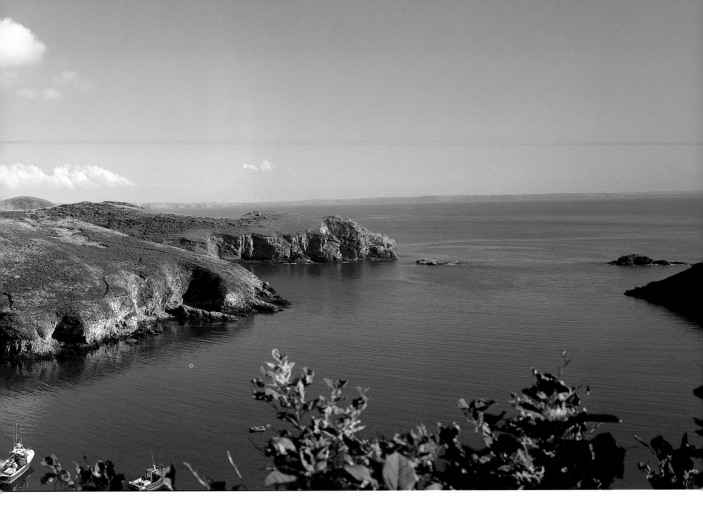

Solva and St David's

The snug harbour at Solva (above) has been a trading port since the 14th century. The magnificent cathedral at nearby St David's (right) occupies a sheltered valley, where earlier structures were built in unsuccessful attempts to hide them from Viking raiders. From Solva, walk westward along the coast path for three miles, to the holy well of St Non, mother of our patron St David, and the ruined chapel where he was born in 462. Continue to the little city of St David's, for a bus back to Solva. Photographers, Duncan Miller, Ken Price (right).

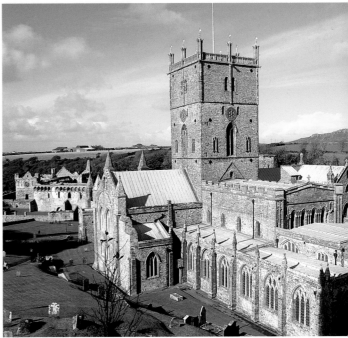

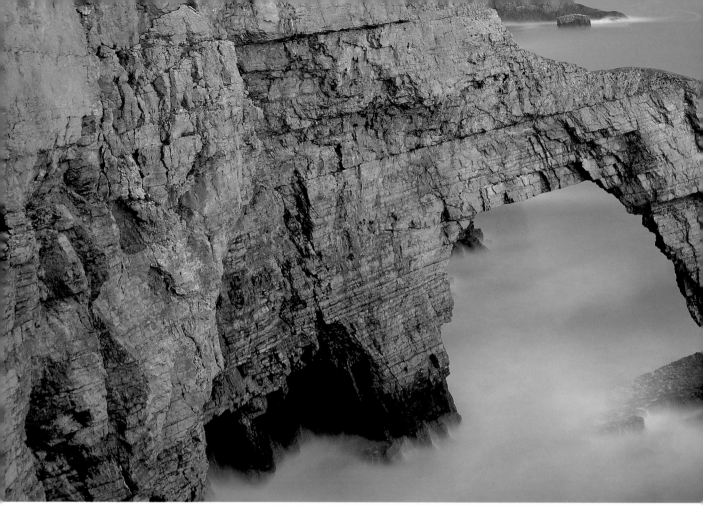

The Green Bridge of Wales

This natural limestone arch on the Castlemartin peninsula soars 80ft above the sea. This, and other arches along this coast, will eventually collapse through erosion, to leave isolated stacks. The definitive National Trail Guide to the Pembrokeshire Coast Path, written by Brian John with support from the Countryside Council for Wales, contains a wealth of information.
Photographer, Aled Hughes.

Seal and kitesurfer

Grey seals are found in abundance around the rocky western coasts of Wales, including Pembrokeshire. Their baleful eyes belie their alertness as they watch the antics of humans – whatever do they make of kitesurfing? Take care, and slow down, if boating in the vicinity of sea caves – these are favourite haunts of seals and you might be rewarded with a glimpse.
Photographer, Andrew Davies.

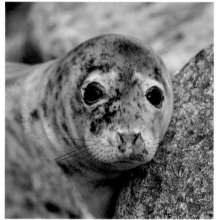

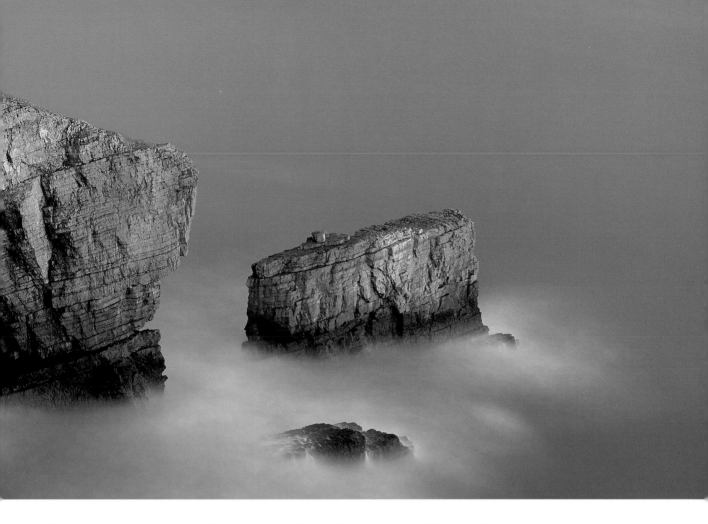

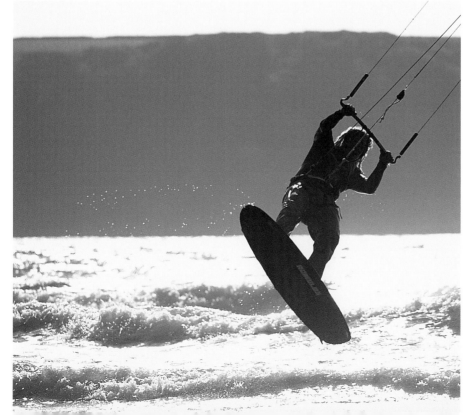

Carmarthenshire

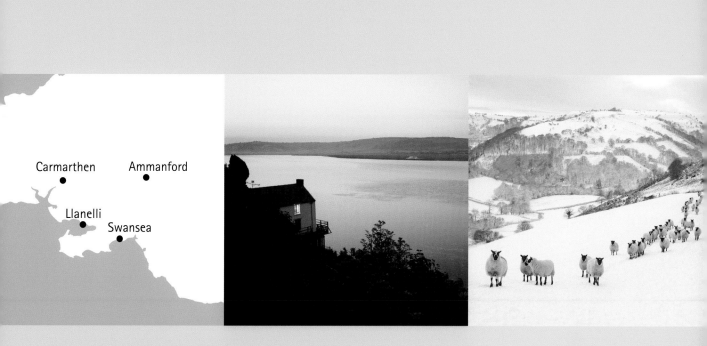

Carmarthen

Ammanford

Llanelli

Swansea

At first sight an industrious region of trucked and tractored agriculture, but also much more than that, Carmarthenshire rewards exploration of its coastline – along with the castles, country parks and historic houses of the verdant Tywi valley.

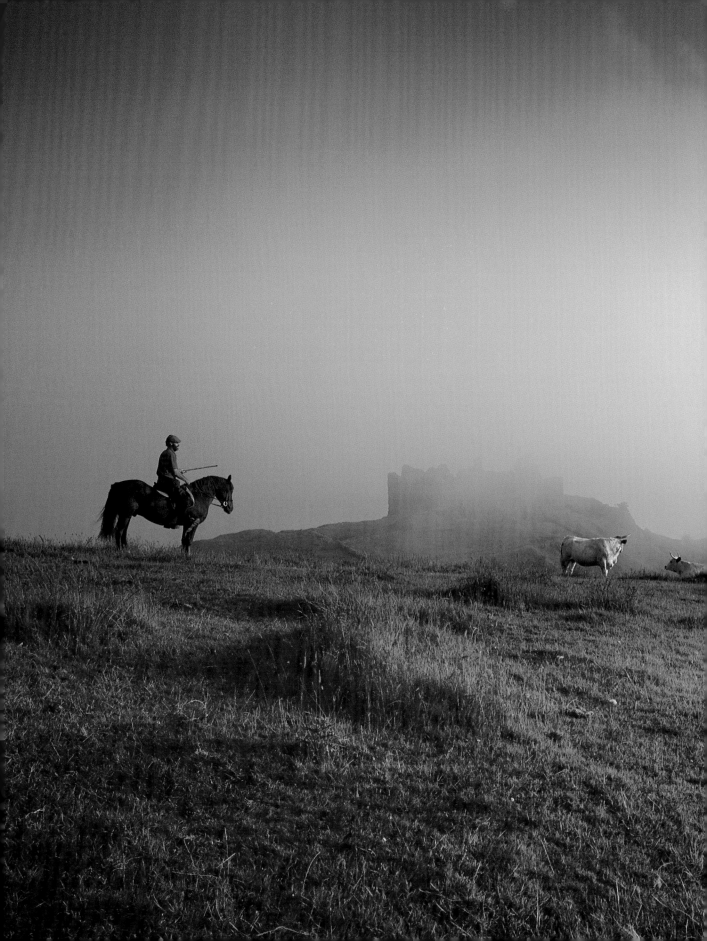

Carreg Cennen Castle
Bernard Llewellyn, custodian of Carreg Cennen Castle and a master of the diversification essential in today's farming economy, looks over his land near Llandeilo. He keeps longhorn cattle and other rare animal breeds, which appear at livestock shows and in historical films. From the A483 south of Llandeilo, follow signs to Trapp and Carreg Cennen Castle, on its precipitous crag.
Photographer, Harry Williams.

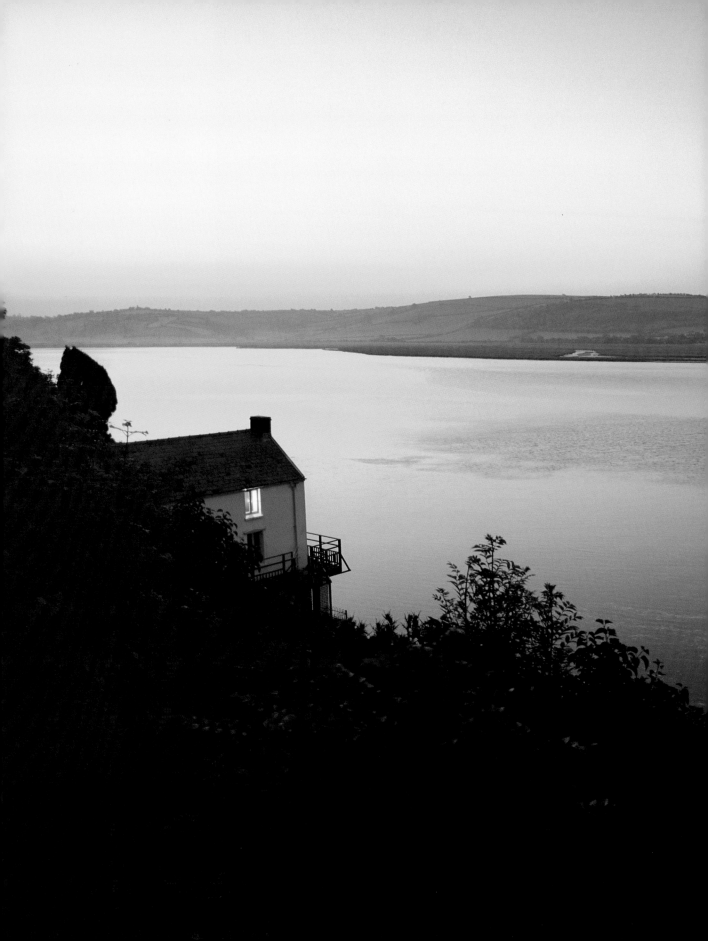

Laugharne, The Boat House
Dylan Thomas's 'seashaken house on a breakneck of rocks' – overlooked by his 'wordsplashed hut' – is now a museum to his life and work. Looking across the 'dabbed bay', it is easy to understand why the sea was such a constant theme in the torrent of genius that poured from his pen. The Dylan Thomas Trail leads you to Laugharne Castle, Brown's Hotel and the simple graves of Dylan and his wife Caitlin in St Martin's Church. Photographer, Harry Williams.

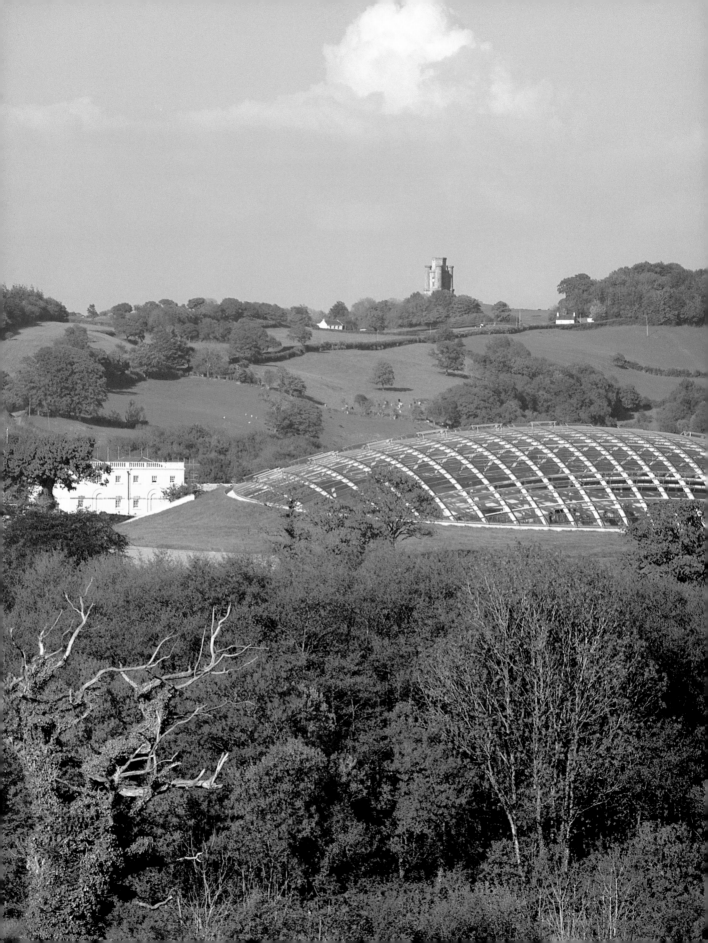

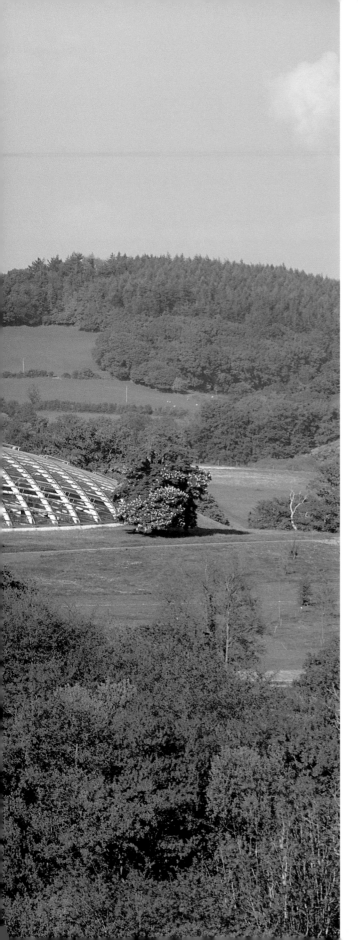

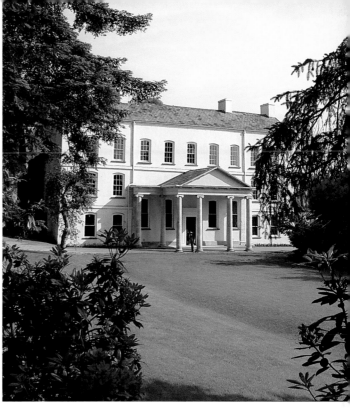

National Botanic Garden of Wales

Set in the gardens and parkland of Middleton Hall, Llanarthne, this botanical showpiece is a feast for the senses. Highlights include the Japanese garden, the walled garden and the Great Glasshouse, designed by Sir Norman Foster, which contains plants from tropical and desert habitats. Leave the A48, between the M4 and Carmarthen, at the garden's own junction – be sure also to see 'the garden lost in time' at nearby Aberglasney. Photographer, Steve Benbow.

Aberglasney

Wales is blessed with several outstandingly fine gardens, created and nurtured by the owners of historic houses and now open for everyone to enjoy. From Bodnant Garden in the Conwy Valley to Dyffryn Gardens near Cardiff, and Aberglasney in Carmarthenshire, they provide an ever-changing spectrum of colour from springtime through to autumn. Aberglasney, at Llangathen, and the National Botanic Garden of Wales are both accessible from the A40 between Carmarthen and Llandeilo.
Photographers,
Janet and Colin Bord.

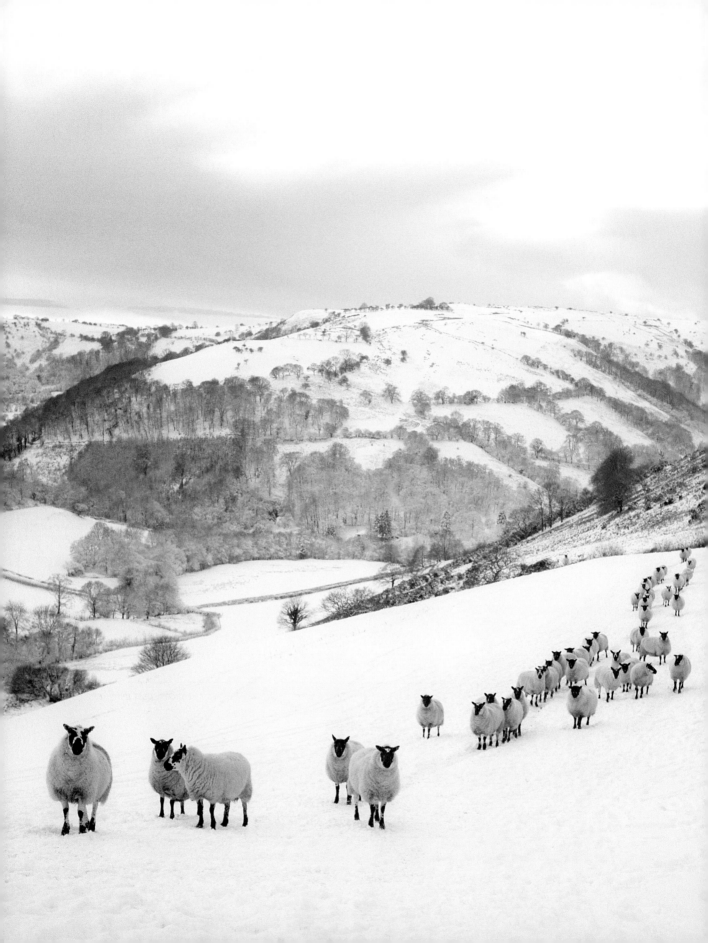

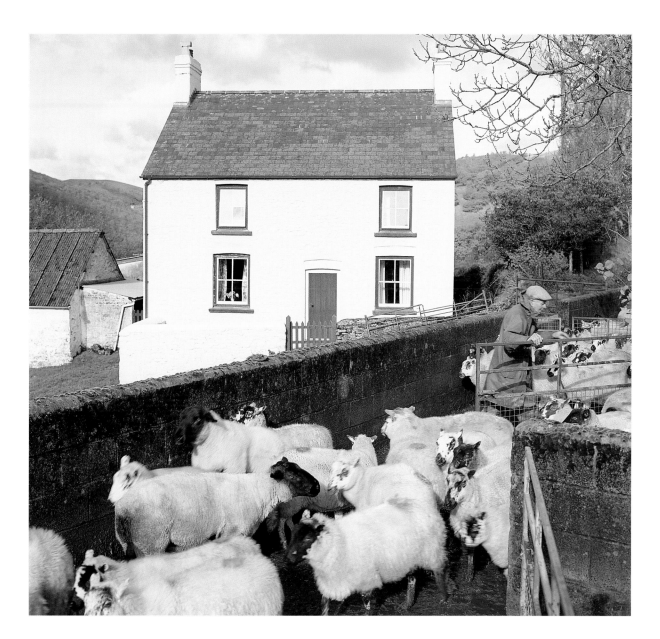

Llandovery
Upland Carmarthenshire,
in the western part of the
Brecon Beacons National
Park, has open countryside,
high moors, glittering lakes
and abundant fresh air
at any time of year.
Visit Myddfai to learn about
the famous physicians,
descendants of the legendary
Lady of the Lake, and their
healing skills.
Photographer, Kathy de Witt.

Sheep farm
Take care driving in rural
Wales – you are likely to
encounter flocks of sheep on
the move. Stop and wait as
they flow past, gently
polishing your car as they go.
Seek out the statue of a
cattle drover at Llandovery.
In the days before road and
rail transport, he and his like
– and their snapping corgis –
would walk cattle and sheep
to market in Bristol or
London, past many a
Drover's Arms.
Photographer, Kathy de Witt.

167

Gower

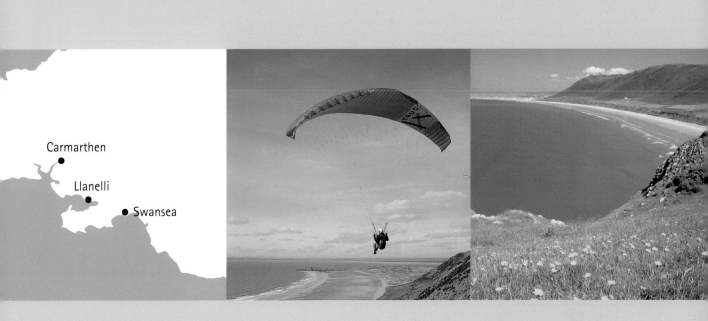

The Gower peninsula was the UK's first designated Area of Outstanding Natural Beauty. From the Victorian resort of Mumbles to the perfect sandy beaches and unspoilt countryside, this is a great place to get away from it all.

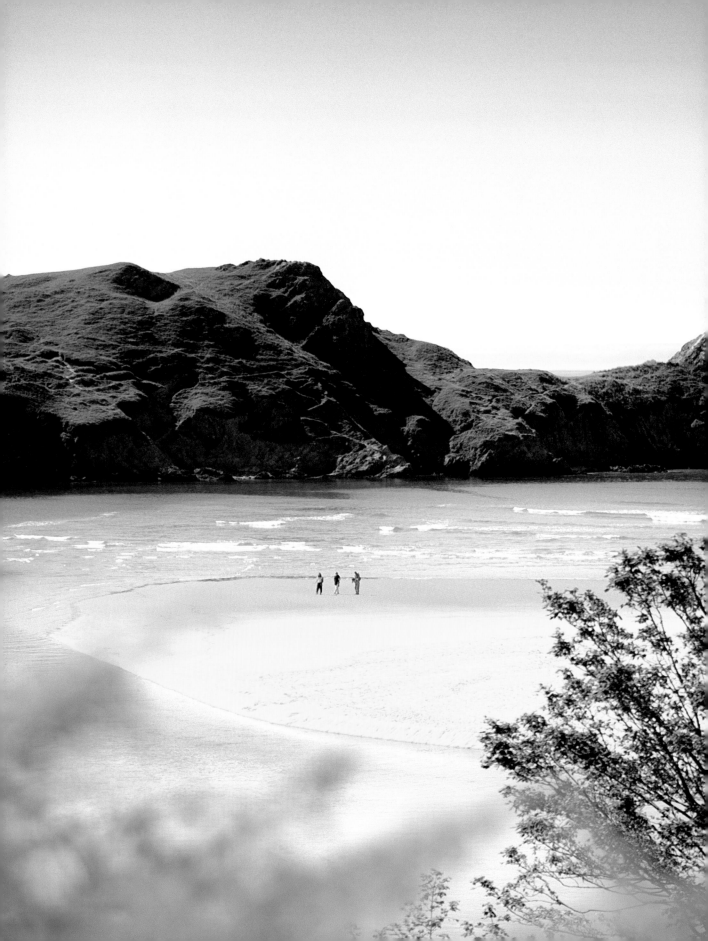

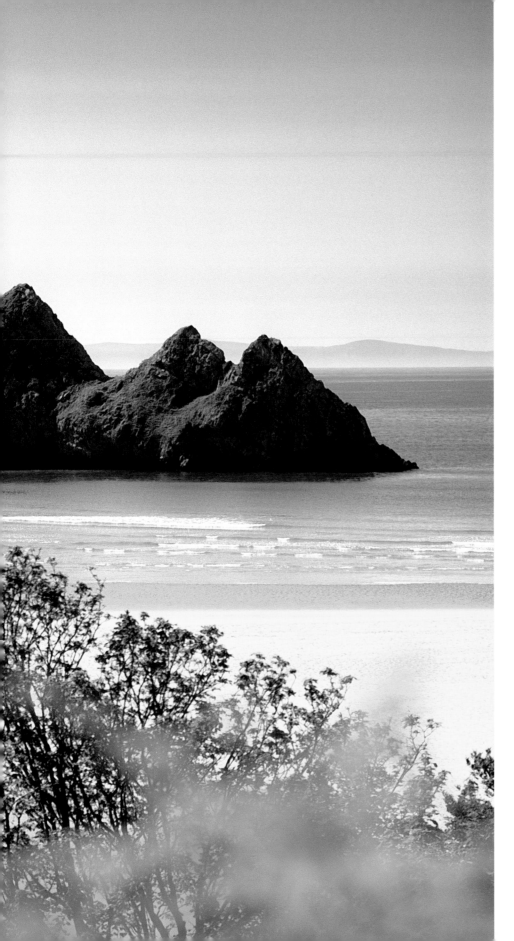

Three Cliffs Bay
It would be difficult to devise a more picturesque beach. Three Cliffs Bay is one of many in Wales to receive a European Blue Flag for their amenities and cleanliness. Follow the A4118 from Swansea to the marvellous beaches at Mumbles, Langland, Caswell Bay, Three Cliffs Bay, Oxwich and Port Eynon. Photographer, Billy Stock.

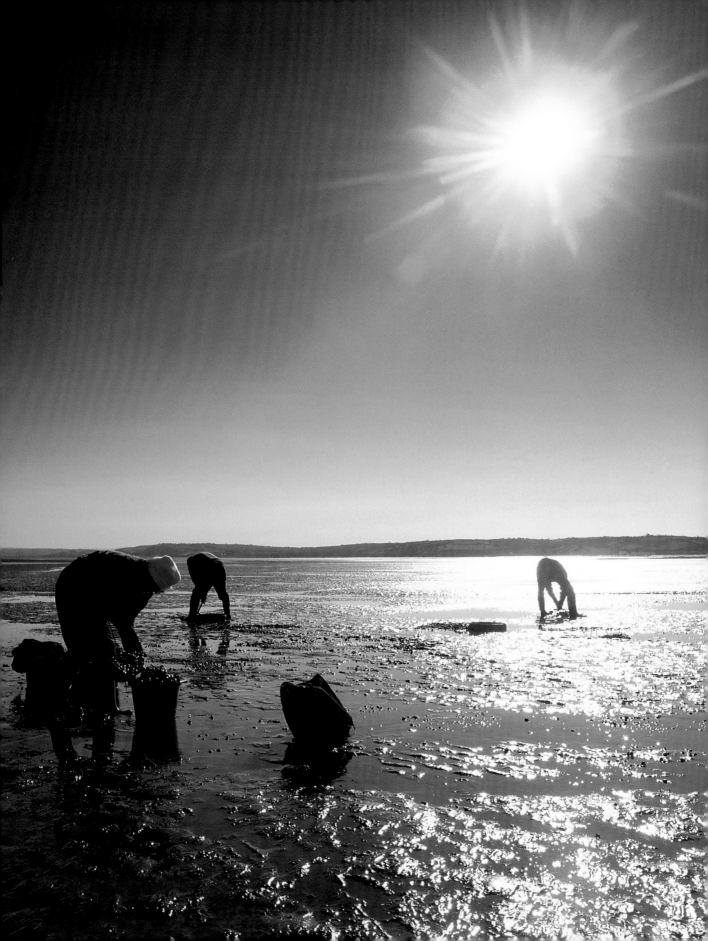

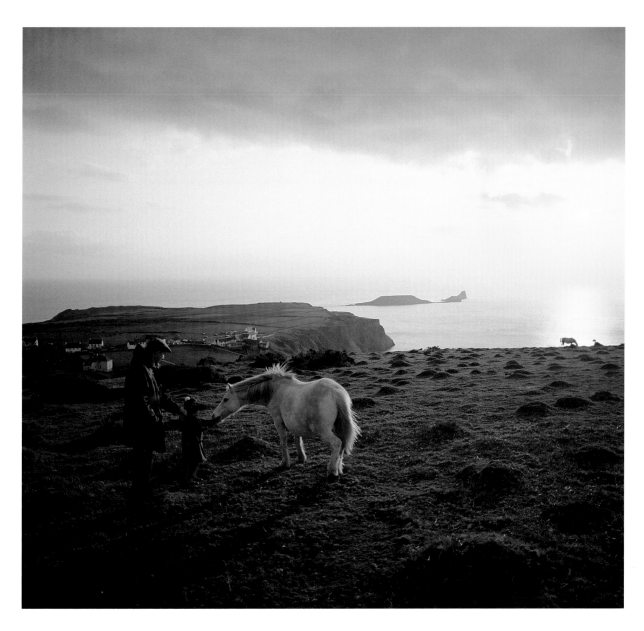

Penclawdd
The traditional, back-straining work of cockle picking continues at Penclawdd on the Loughor estuary. Seafood features strongly at the Swansea Food Festival each October, and is skilfully presented at restaurants in Mumbles and elsewhere. Pop into Swansea's excellent indoor market and pick up the ingredients for Gower's quintessential breakfast – cockles, bacon and laverbread (an edible seaweed) served with toast. Photographer, Harry Williams.

Rhossili
Gower is a maze of footpaths and bridlepaths waiting to be explored. The high cliffs convey a tremendous sense of space – and are great places to enjoy feeling windswept. Maps showing walks and cycle tracks are available locally – the Celtic Trail (National Cycle Network route 4) passes by. Photographer, Harry Williams.

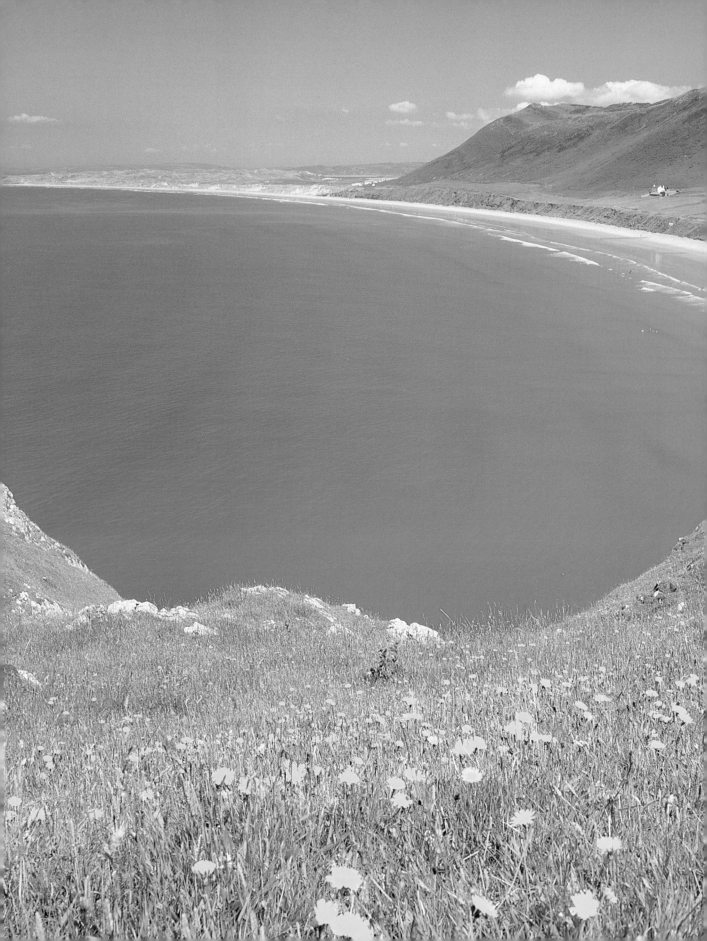

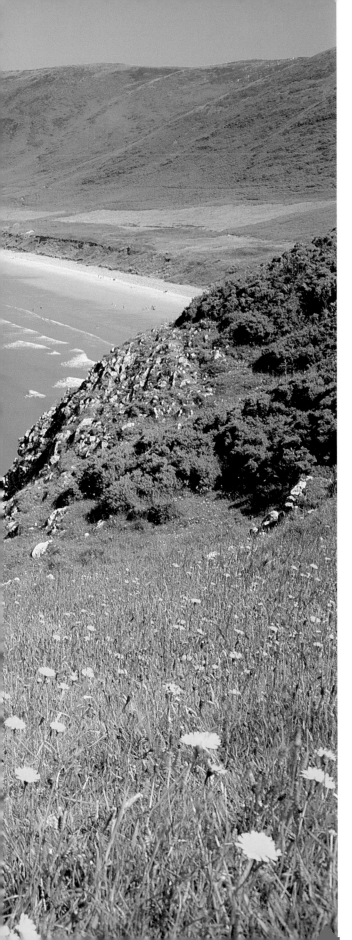

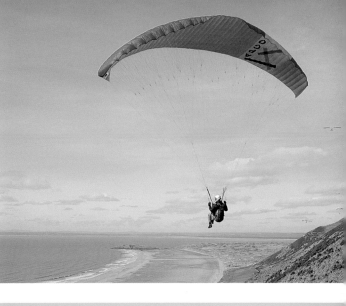

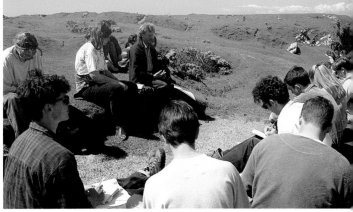

Rhossili

For surfing, windsurfing –
and paragliding from the
hills behind – this long
sweep of sand at the tip
of Gower, open to winds
and Atlantic swell from the
west, takes some beating.
From Swansea Bay's long
promenades to Gower's
clifftop paths and beach
campsites, this entire region
enables you to get close to
the sea – using as much or
as little energy as you wish.
Photographers, Billy Stock
(left) and Chris Warren.

Field studies

The coastal and lowland
heath habitats are rich in
plant, bird and animal life –
as this study group is
learning. Special interest
breaks – to study wildlife,
photography, painting,
cooking, gardening or crafts –
are popular.
Photographer, Andrew Davies.

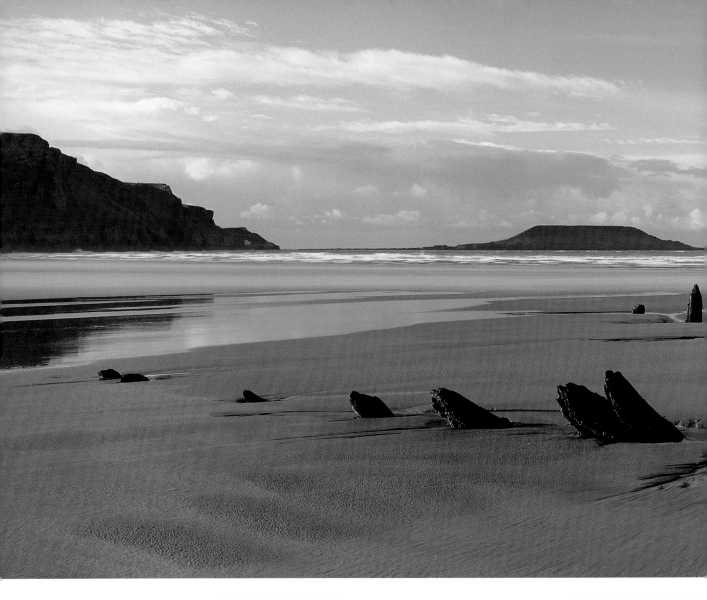

Wreck of the Helvetia

Worm's Head, in the distance, was named by the Vikings – after their word for a dragon. The schooner Helvetia was inward bound for Swansea with a cargo of Canadian timber, when she was blown ashore at Rhossili. Park at the top of the cliff and walk down to Rhossili beach – the timbers of the wreck are exposed at low water.

Photographer, Aled Hughes.

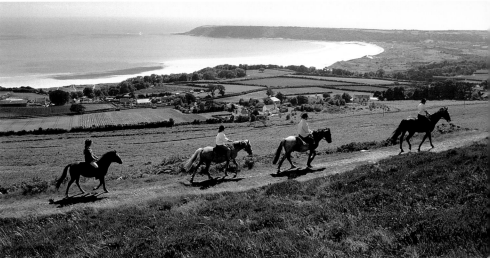

Photographer, Andrew Orchard.

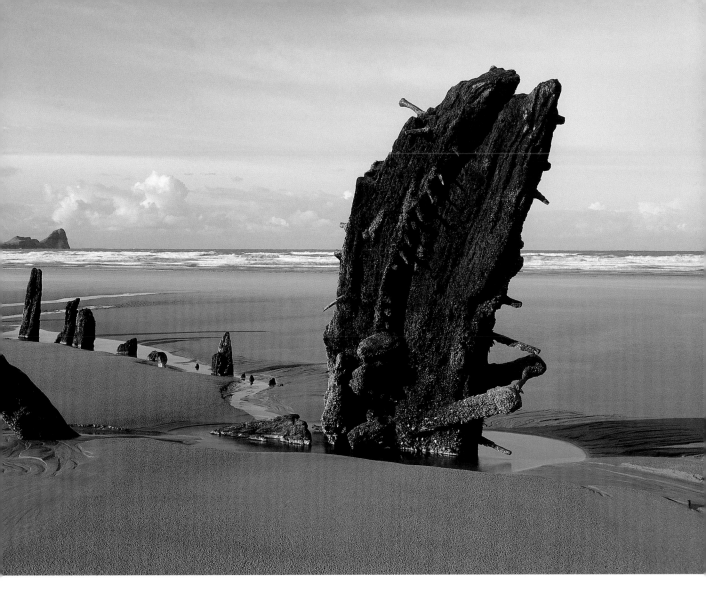

Get active

Whether you seek the views and camaraderie of pony trekking or the adrenalin rush of riding the perfect wave, Gower is an accessible place to connect with the joys, or the forces, of nature. Riding and trekking stables are plentiful – and westward-facing beaches produce perfectly formed surf when conditions are right.
Photographer, Steve Benbow.

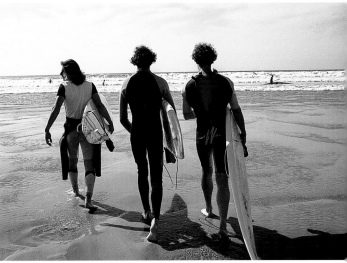

Cardiff and the Vale of Glamorgan

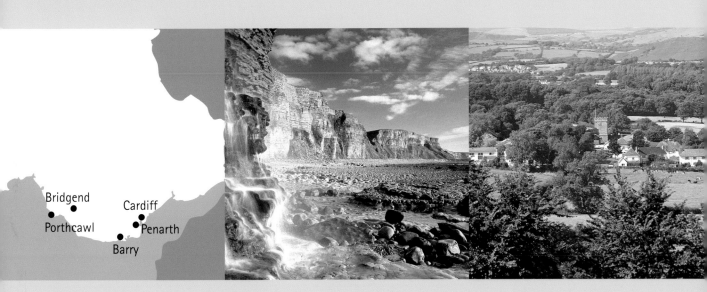

Bridgend
Porthcawl
Barry
Cardiff
Penarth

This pleasant and fruitful landscape, appreciated since Roman times by those seeking a comfortable place to live, continues to be popular as a peaceful and stylish retreat immediately west of our capital city, Cardiff.

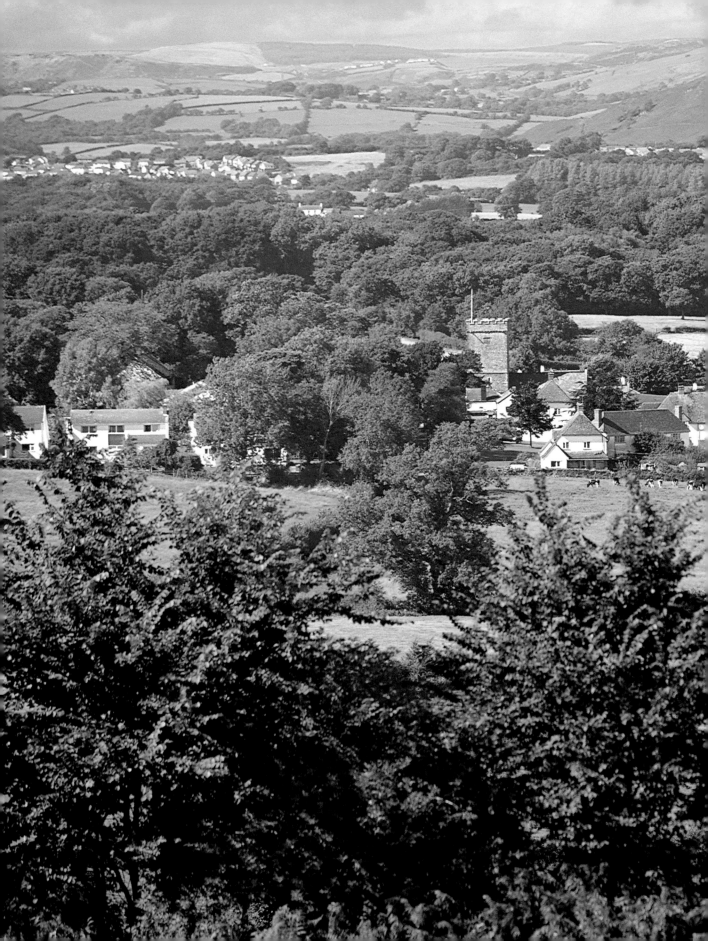

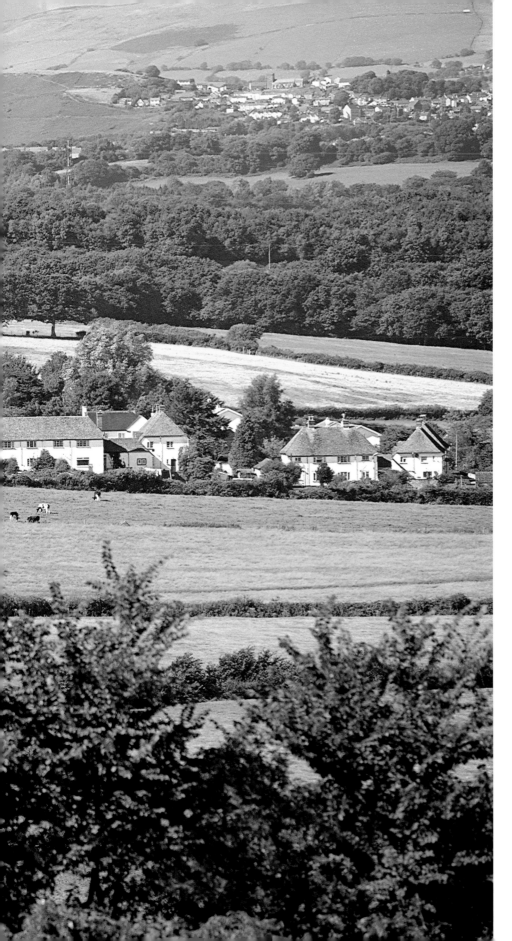

Pendoylan
The Vale of Glamorgan is a place of leafy lanes and cosy villages. Wales's leading vineyard – Llanerch – is near here. See the rows of vines at Llanerch Vineyard, close to Junction 34 on the M4 – and try the award-winning, and most agreeable, wines.
Photographer, Steve Benbow.

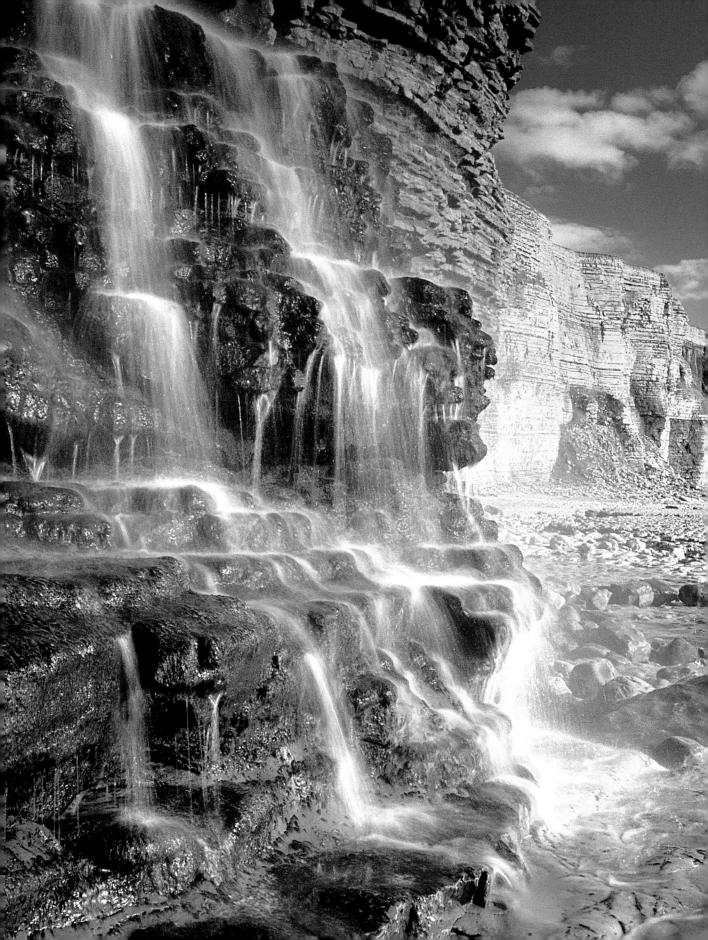

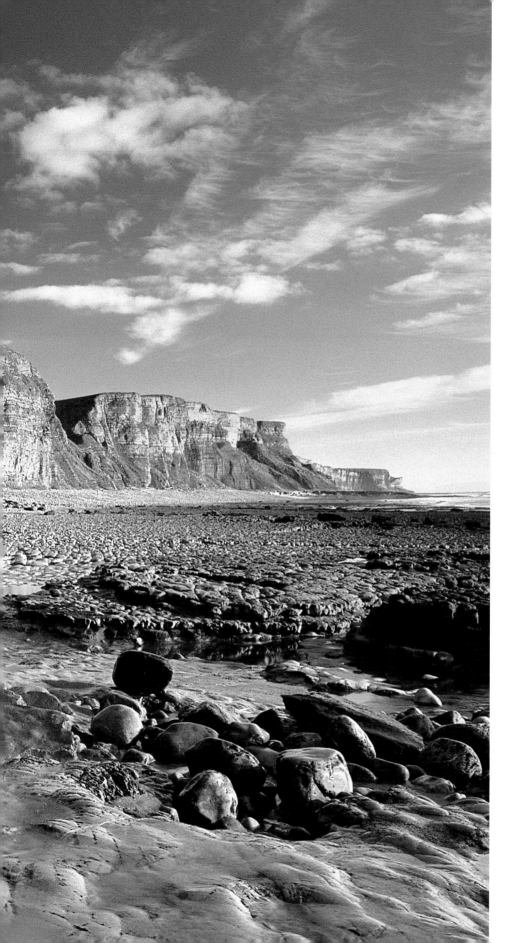

Dunraven Bay
The Glamorgan Heritage Coast, which extends from St Athan to the Merthyr Mawr sand dune system, a Site of Special Scientific Interest, is characterised by dramatic, clearly stratified, sandstone cliffs and breathtaking views. Call at the Heritage Coast visitor centre at Southerndown to learn about the geology and wildlife.
Photographer, Jeremy Moore.

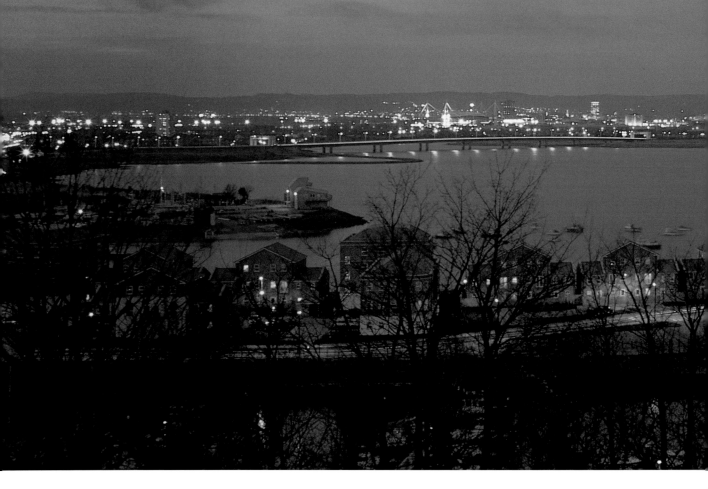

Cardiff Bay

Cardiff grew where coal-mining valleys converged upon a sheltered bay destined, a century ago, to become the world's largest coal-exporting port. The revitalised Cardiff Bay – home to the National Assembly for Wales – now provides a thriving business and cultural environment, helping to equip Cardiff for a confident future as the capital city of Wales. Take a walk along the Cardiff Bay Barrage, from the car park near Penarth Marina. Look inland toward the valleys, then out to sea, to understand how the landscape determined the position of this dynamic city.

Photographer, Chris Colclough.

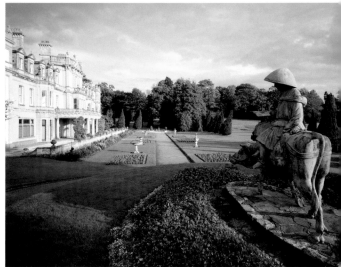

184

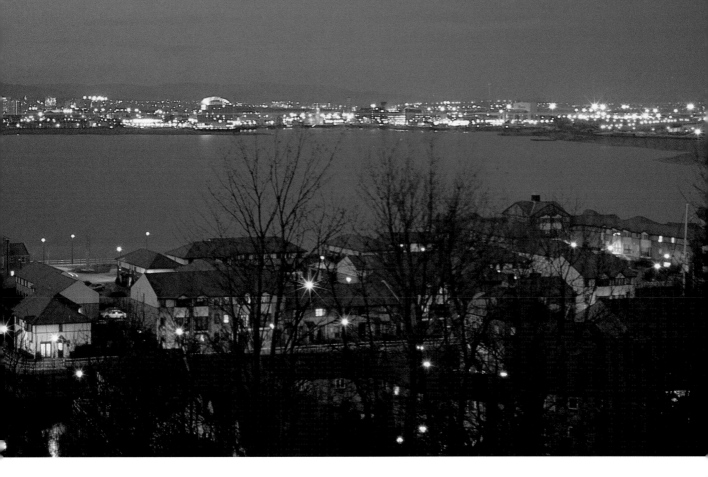

Dyffryn Gardens

One of the finest and largest of Wales's landscaped gardens lies between Cardiff and Cowbridge. Some seventy acres of Grade-1 listed Edwardian gardens and parkland, including themed areas and formal terraces, are open to the public. Follow signs from St Nicholas, on the A48 west of Cardiff, to Dyffryn Gardens – shrubs and seasonal flower beds erupt in blazes of colour, and reward repeat visits. Photographer, Chris Colclough.

Museum of Welsh Life, St Fagans

This is one of Europe's leading open-air museums. A fascinating collection of buildings, transported from all over Wales and authentically rebuilt, shows how people lived from 1500 onwards. This is the Aber-Nodwydd farmhouse, built at Llangadfan, Powys, in 1678. St Fagan's is near Junction 33 on the M4 motorway west of Cardiff. Photographer, Andrew Davies.

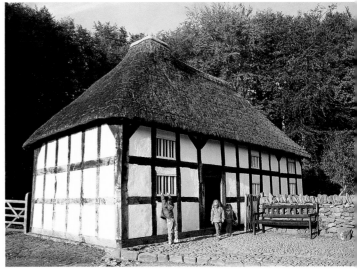

Severn, Wye and Usk

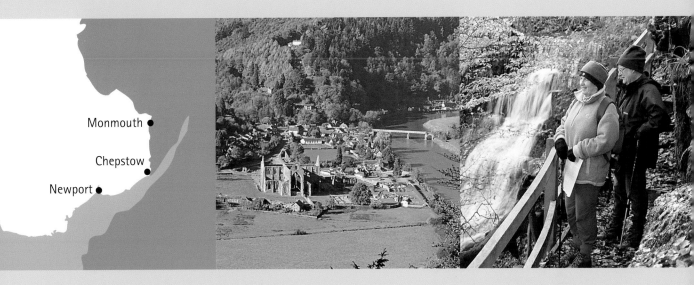

Three of Wales's rivers converge in the south-east.
The Severn has two majestic bridges over its broad
estuary. The Wye, having meandered easily through
placid borderlands, cuts through a dramatic gorge
at Tintern. The Usk, the longest river to flow entirely
within Wales, reaches the sea at Newport.

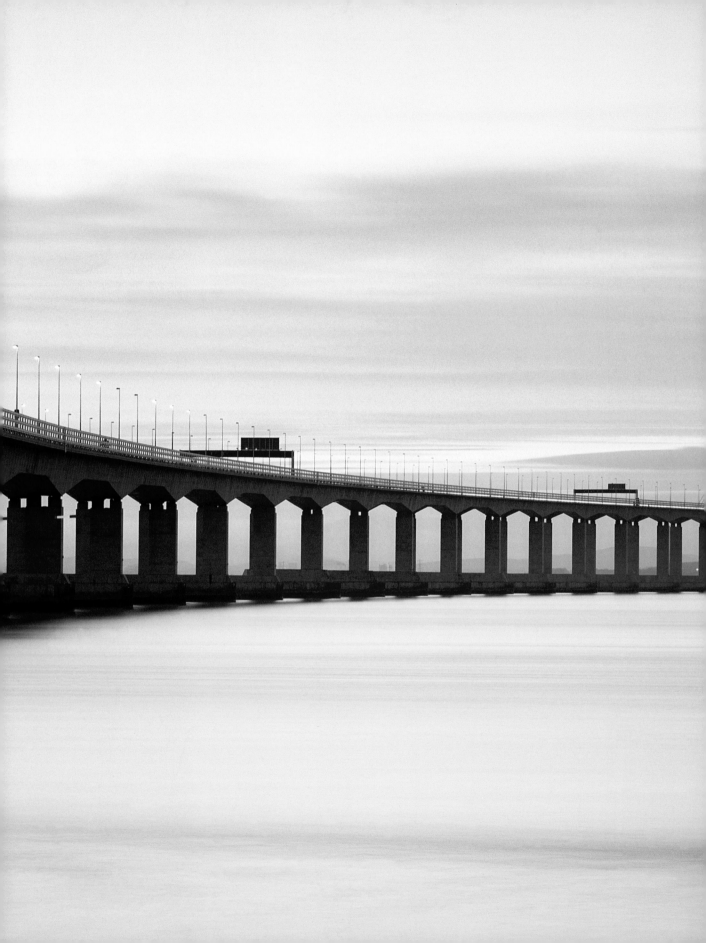

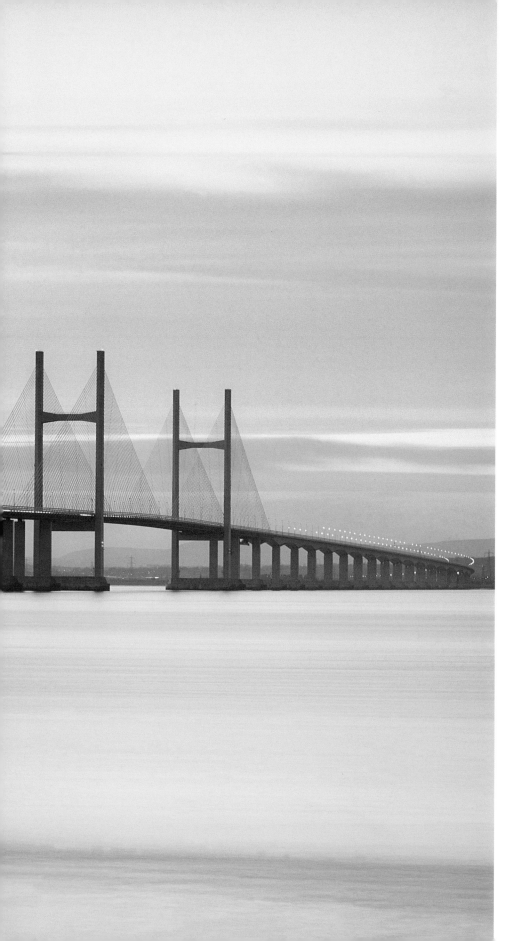

Second Severn Crossing
The newer of the two road bridges over the Severn estuary symbolises the economic links between Wales and the rest of the UK and Europe. Tourists, truckers and sports fans – and Welsh people returning home – understand, as they cross, that they are arriving somewhere special. Drive over both Severn bridges to experience the wide seascapes or take the foot and cycle path over the older bridge from Severn View services. Photographer, Billy Stock.

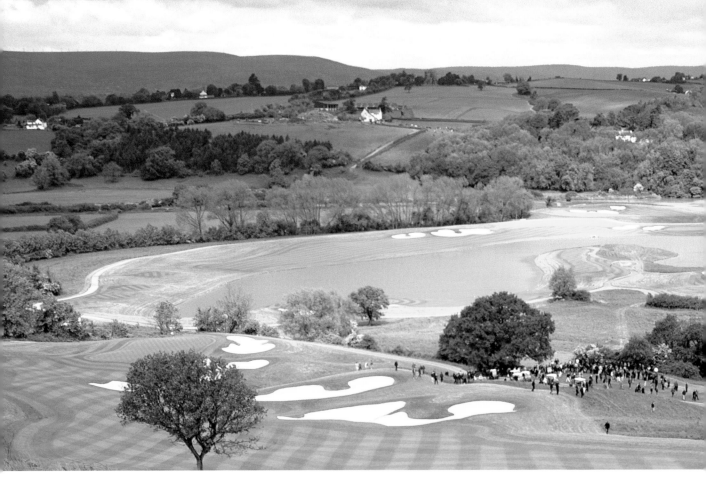

Celtic Manor Resort

The Wentwood Hills golf course at the Celtic Manor Resort, Newport – bounded by the meandering Usk – will host the sport's most prestigious competition, the Ryder Cup, in 2010. For non-golfers – countryside rangers have devised waymarked trails, and will take you on guided walks, in Wentwood Forest. Photographer, Andy Stoyle.

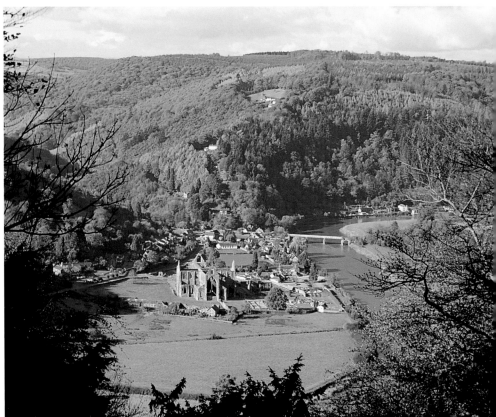

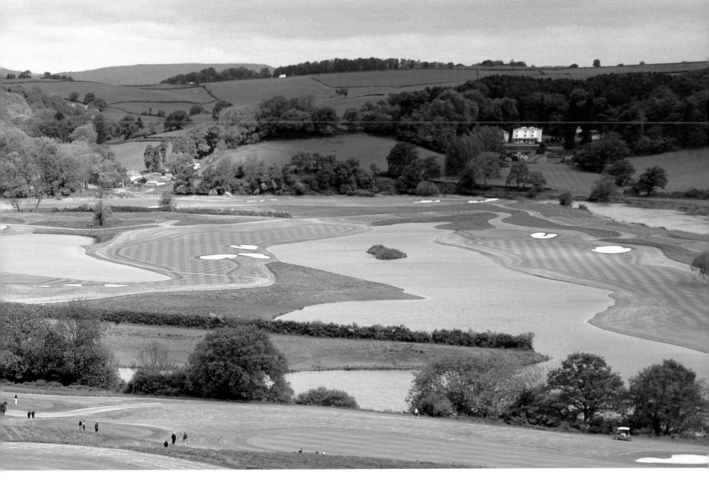

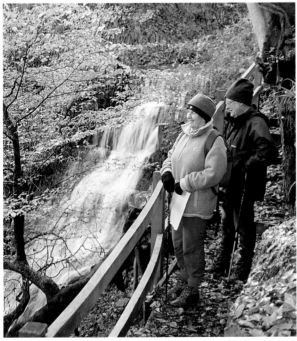

**Tintern Abbey and
Cleddon Falls**
Immortalised in verse by
Wordsworth, and on canvas
by Turner and countless
other artists, the ruins of
the 11th-century Cistercian
abbey at Tintern add historic
dignity to this most
picturesque of valleys,
with its maze of footpaths
first trodden by Victorian
tourists. Acquire a copy of
Wordsworth's, 'Lines
composed a few miles above
Tintern Abbey', and find a
peaceful spot, within sight
of the Wye, to read and
absorb his profound words.
Photographer, David Williams.

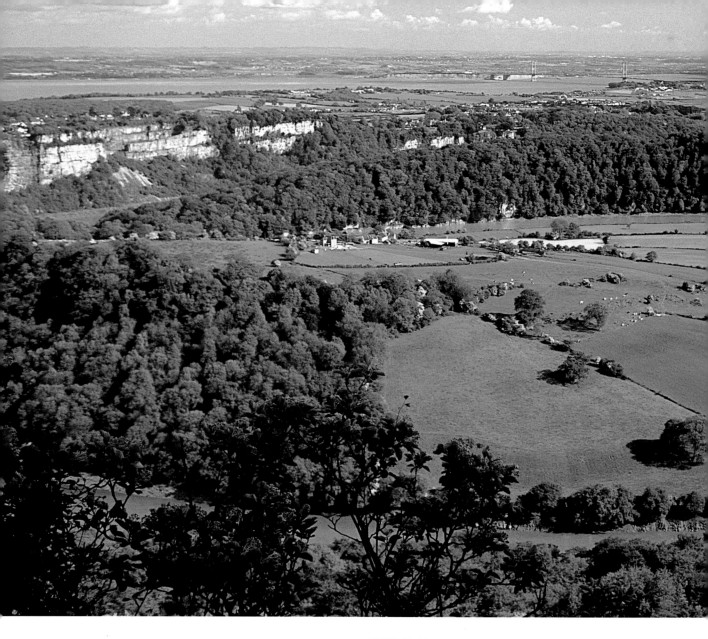

Wye Valley from Wyndcliffe
High, wooded cliffs a couple of miles south of Tintern Abbey look out over a bend in the river Wye toward Chepstow, the Severn bridges and the Bristol Channel. Leave the A466 where it bends sharply just north of St Arvans (signposted Wyndcliffe) and follow a lane to a car park – from which a pleasant walk through woodland leads to the thrilling Eagle's Nest viewpoint.
Photographer, Jeremy Moore.

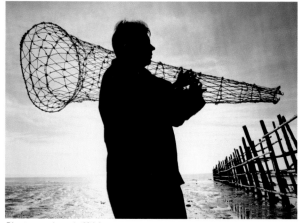

Photographer, Jeff Morgan.

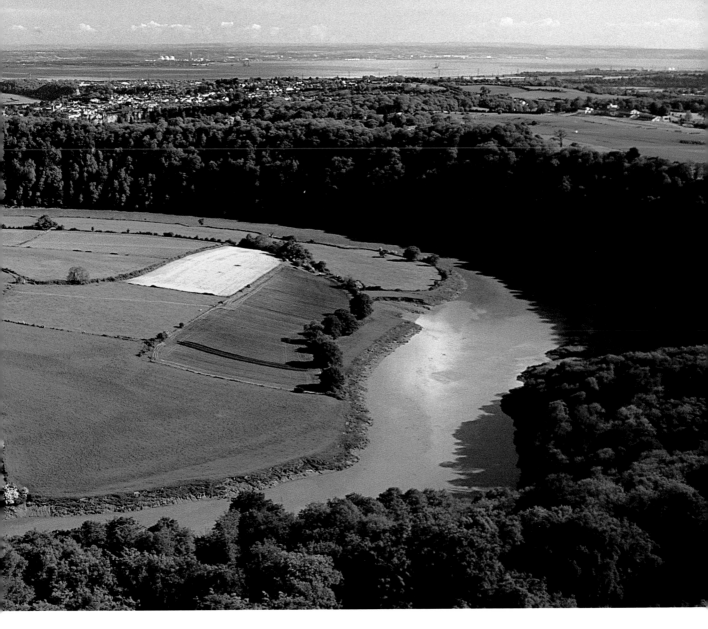

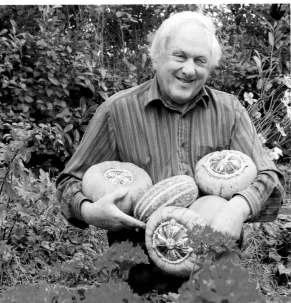

Land of plenty
The market gardens, orchards, dairies, smokeries, vineyards and traditional fisheries of this corner of Wales produce a wealth of high-quality produce, from the familiar to the unexpected. Farmers' markets are held twice-monthly at Monmouth, Chepstow and Usk. Photographer, Rex Moreton.

The Geology of Wales

The landscape of Wales is a product of over 700 million years of evolution, involving numerous and continuous physical and biological changes. Our oldest known rocks in the region were formed when southern Britain, including Wales, was part of a vast supercontinent named Gondwana, situated in the southern hemisphere far south of the equator. Following the break-up of the supercontinent, the fragments of the Earth's crust that now make up Wales drifted across the globe to their present position at temperate latitudes in the northern hemisphere. This amazing journey through time involved crossing different latitudes and different environments, from which much of the evidence is locked up in the rocks and fossils beneath our feet, and which in turn are the basis for our remarkably diverse and often spectacular scenery.

Areas of the oldest rocks are best displayed across much of Anglesey and western Llŷn, in eastern Powys extending into the adjacent borderlands, and in north Pembrokeshire. The intensely distorted cliffs in the South Stack area of Holy Island, Anglesey, are stunningly visual examples of folding and faulting that have affected such rocks in response to the huge forces involved in the processes of plate tectonics and continental drift that even now drive the crust of our planet in constant motion.

Between about 550 million and 420 million years ago, Wales was mostly under the sea as it drifted across the equator into the tropics of the northern hemisphere. Vast amounts of sand, silt and mud accumulated in the ocean, preserved today in the bleak sandstone moorlands of the Harlech Dome and the slate quarries of north Wales, and in the beautiful cliffs along the Pembrokeshire Coastal Path to the south of St David's. Then we literally collided with other continents, first the Scandinavian-Russian block and then the north American mass that included Greenland. The collision events resulted in massive volcanic eruptions, both on land and underwater. These produced the rocks that now form much of Snowdonia and the Aran mountains, including Snowdon itself and Cadair Idris, together with related areas around Builth Wells and north Pembrokeshire – where Strumble Head mirrors areas of the world such as Hawaii, which is subject today to similar oceanic volcanicity.

Meanwhile, towards the end of this period there were coral reefs forming in the shallow seas around the eastern margins of Wales, now seen in the Usk area and up into the borderlands in environments that were not too different from the present-day Caribbean. Uplift from the sea, involving long periods of mountain building and erosion, then saw Wales as part of a desert landmass that stretched from present-day north America across northern Europe to Russia. Until about 350 million years ago, extensive river systems drained from the Brecon Beacons, together with the rich red soils that blanket much of the borderland. The red sandstone cliffs of Manorbier, Barafundle and Milford Haven in Pembrokeshire, and parts of eastern Anglesey are also remnants of this ancient landmass.

Then the warm, subtropical sea invaded yet again, spreading lime-rich sediments with abundant corals around the margins of the country. In north Wales, the Great Orme and Little Orme headlands at Llandudno, and the Eglwyseg escarpment near Llangollen, are formed of the massive limestones resulting from these deposits. In the south, the beautiful sea cliffs of Gower and of the Castlemartin coast, with its spectacular blow-holes and the Green Bridge of Wales arch, are preserved in the same rocks. Eventually the shallow seas silted up with sand and mud carried in rivers from the uplands of central Wales to form large deltas and low coastal plains in both the north and the south. On these swampy plains grew lush, subtropical vegetation – not unlike the Florida Everglades of today. At intervals the dense plant cover was drowned by brief incursions of the sea, killing off the vegetation to form thick deposits of peat. This pattern was repeated in numerous cycles and the peat beds were buried and compressed, eventually being transformed into the coal seams now preserved in the coalfields of the north-east and south.

About 300 million years ago the great coal forests were destroyed, when renewed uplift again turned Wales into a mountainous desert region. Eventually dinosaurs and early mammals were to colonise parts of this land, but most of the rocks have been removed by later erosion, apart from small areas in the Vale of Clwyd and on the south-east Glamorgan coast. The distinctive creamy-coloured horizontal limestone cliffs of south Glamorgan, running from Penarth to Ogmore, are remnants of another shallow marine invasion that began 200 million years ago and which may have spread more widely across the eroded land.

After this time there is very little record of solid rocks preserved in Wales. By about 65 million years ago we had drifted north from the tropics, more or less to our present location, and the modern Atlantic Ocean had opened, introducing our temperate maritime climate. The area was now finally emergent from the sea, and repeated pulses of uplift and erosion saw the establishment of the basic patterns of modern landforms and of the river drainage system. In brief, Wales was approaching its modern outline by 2 million years ago.

Then, however, came one further set of dramatic events – beginning 1.6 million years ago – which were to play a major role in the final shaping of the Welsh landscape. This was the great Ice Age, which lasted until just 13,000 years ago. There were repeated glaciations with milder interglacial periods. At its maximum extent the ice cover advanced southwards to about the Brecon Beacons, with a major glacier system also in the Irish Sea. All marginal areas were deeply frozen in Siberia-like tundra scenery, and the animal life included mammoth, bison, reindeer, wolf and arctic hare.

The great north Wales glaciers carved out the deep U-shaped valleys, such as Nant Ffrancon and Nant Peris, together with the numerous cwms and peaks throughout Snowdonia and neighbouring areas. Many of the dramatic mountain ridges were produced by frost shattering in the prolonged icy-cold climate. The huge amounts of rock eroded by the glaciers were eventually dumped as boulder trails over much of the landscape – and many of our lakes were formed as a result of deep scouring by ice. With so much water locked up in the ice, one other striking feature of the Ice Age was a major fall in sea level, by about as much as 100 metres, so that our surrounding seas disappeared. The Irish Sea and Bristol Channel became dry land, and there was also direct connection into Europe via a dry English Channel and North Sea. When the ice finally melted, the sea re-invaded these areas, drowning the coastal valleys such as Solva, the Severn estuary, Milford Haven and the Menai Strait, and shaping our modern coastline.

On land, streams and rivers draining from the melting glaciers carried vast amounts of rock and soil debris across the landscape in a blanket cover that forms much of the rolling scenery of central Wales, and which in no small part now determines the patterns of vegetation and agriculture.

Since the Ice Age, warmer-climate plants and animals have invaded Wales from the south – including humans, whose impact on our scenery has been considerable. Over the past 10,000 years much of the natural forest has been stripped as humans moved from existing as nomadic hunter-gatherers to ways of life tied to farming and settlement. From around 2,000 BC onwards, Bronze Age – and later Iron Age – people began to establish the first industrial cultures, and constructed hill forts as major features of the landscape. Then came the Romans with their fortresses and encampments, and their network of roads.

Wales became a distinct nation as its regional rulers united against Saxon and Viking attack, but was partly conquered by the Normans after 1066 and finally overwhelmed by Edward 1 in the late 13th century. His castles, along with those of Welsh princes and Norman invaders, remain today as striking features of our scenery. Examples such as Caerphilly, Carreg Cennen, Pembroke, Harlech, Caernarfon, Dolwyddelan, Conwy and Dinas Brân are telling reminders of the reliance on local supplies of rock in the building of these magnificent edifices.

And so to the industrial revolution of the past few centuries, when the impact of human activity on the landscape has been as visual as the natural processes of the preceding 700 million years. Massive development of the coalfields, the slate-quarrying belts of north Wales, the road and railway networks, the construction of major ports, and the exponential growth of towns and cities are just some of the factors that continue the evolutionary changes to the structure and culture of the country.

Together with the continuing natural, physical and biological changes, the rate of evolution will undoubtedly increase yet further in the future.

Professor Michael G Bassett
National Museums & Galleries of Wales

Index

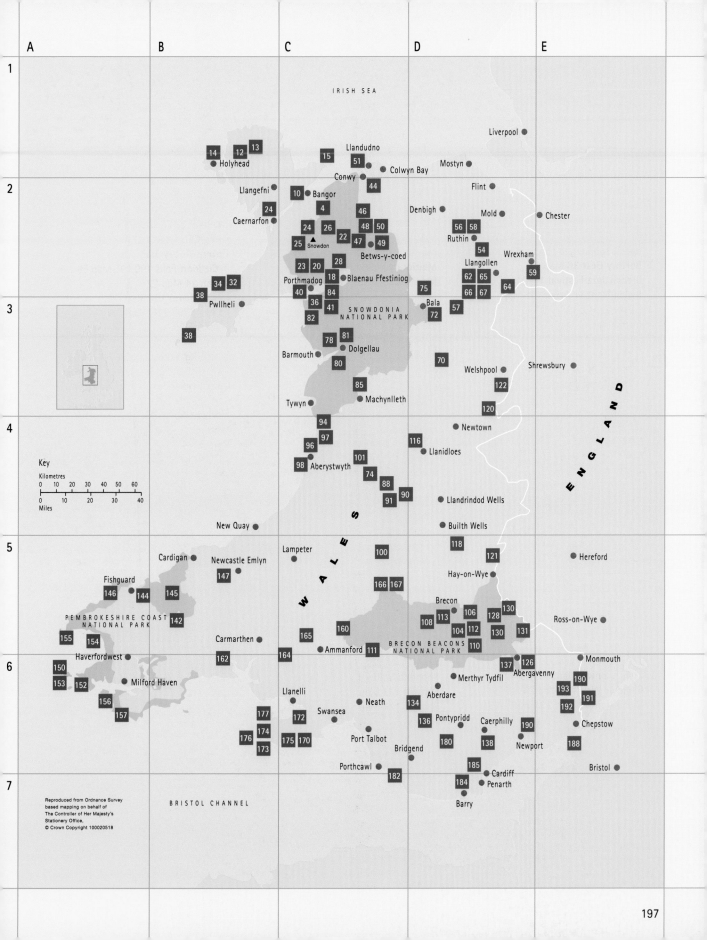

IRISH SEA

14 12 13
● Holyhead

15 Llandudno
51
Colwyn Bay ●
Conwy
44 Mostyn ●
● Liverpool

Llangefni ●
10 ● Bangor
24 4
Caernarfon ●
24 26 46
25 ▲ Snowdon 48 50
22 47
23 20 49
28 Betws-y-coed
18 Blaenau Ffestiniog ●
Porthmadog
40 84
34 32 36 41
38 82
38 Pwllheli ●
78 81
Barmouth ● Dolgellau ●
80

Denbigh ●
Flint ●
Mold ●
Ruthin ● 56 58
54
Llangollen
62 65
66 67 64
75
Bala ●
72 57
70 Welshpool ●
122
120

Chester ●
Wrexham
59

85
Tywyn ● Machynlleth ●

SNOWDONIA
NATIONAL PARK

ENGLAND

94
96 97
98 Aberystwyth ●
101
74
88
91 90

116
Llanidloes ●
● Newtown

Shrewsbury ●

Llandrindod Wells ●

New Quay ●

Key
Kilometres
0 10 20 30 40 50 60
0 10 20 30 40
Miles

Lampeter ●
100

118

● Builth Wells

121
● Hereford

Cardigan ●
Newcastle Emlyn ●
147

166 167
Hay-on-Wye ●

W
A
L
E
S

Fishguard ●
146 144 145
142
PEMBROKESHIRE COAST
NATIONAL PARK
155 154
Haverfordwest ●
150
153 152
● Milford Haven
156
157

Carmarthen ●
162

165
160
164
Ammanford ●
111

108 113 Brecon ●
106
104 112
110
128 130
130 131

BRECON BEACONS
NATIONAL PARK

137 126
Abergavenny ●
● Monmouth
190
193
192 191

Ross-on-Wye ●

Llanelli ●
172 Swansea ●
176 174
175 170
177
173

● Neath

Port Talbot ●
Bridgend ●
Porthcawl ●
182

134
Aberdare ●
136 Pontypridd ●
180

● Merthyr Tydfil

Caerphilly ●
138
190
Newport ●

188

Chepstow ●
● Bristol

185 ● Cardiff
184 ● Penarth
● Barry

BRISTOL CHANNEL

Reproduced from Ordnance Survey
based mapping on behalf of
The Controller of Her Majesty's
Stationery Office,
© Crown Copyright 100020518

197

Wales – facts and figures

Wales is one of the ancient Celtic lands of western Europe. Its central landscape of hills, mountains and river valleys is bounded on three sides by fertile lowlands and a spectacular coastline - and on the fourth by the green shires of England.

The climate is temperate – the warm waters of the Gulf Stream moderate the weather, which is mild compared with other places at similar latitude.

The landscape contains a wealth of archaeological evidence telling the story of the people who have lived here since prehistoric times. Stone-age sites and monuments abound, especially in Anglesey and Pembrokeshire.

In 1997, the Welsh people voted for a measure of devolved government, separate from Parliament in London. Today, the National Assembly for Wales applies its powers to matters of education, health, transport, local government, culture and economic development within Wales.

The Welsh language, which evolved from the Celtic language spoken over much of Britain in pre-Saxon times, has official status alongside English. It is spoken by around half a million people, is taught in schools and studied in our universities, and supports a thriving culture. There are Welsh-language television and radio services – and our famous enthusiasm for music, literature and poetry reaches its peak each summer at the National Eisteddfod.

The Welsh economy benefits from a skilled workforce and an excellent education system. The traditional heavy industries, including coal and steel, have been superseded by science, technology and service industries. Leading-edge companies in information technology, energy, agriculture and biotechnology work in close association with the research departments of our universities.

Tourism and agriculture sustain many of the people who live in the places featured in this book. The upland areas support sheep farming and a wide range of leisure pursuits, while the rich soils of the lowlands and coastal plains tend to be given over to cattle or arable farming – along with gentler holiday activity. Visitors find the countryside and towns of Wales accessible, safe, friendly and fascinating.

On account of its incomparable landscape, welcoming inhabitants, first-rate education system, favourable economic climate and excellent communications, Wales is recognised as providing a quality of life which is second to none.

Population
2,903,100 – of whom 16% speak, read and write Welsh fluently, and 24% can understand the language.
Source – 2001 census, published 2003.

Area
20,640 square km – some 8,000 square miles.

About 60 per cent of our coastal waters are designated by the European Union as being of European importance in conservation terms.

Eleven per cent of our land surface is categorised as being of national importance for nature conservation.

Wales has over 1,000 Sites of Special Scientific Interest - and almost 25% of our land surface is either National Park or Area of Outstanding Natural Beauty.

Dimensions
Around 160 miles from north to south, between 50 and 120 miles from west to east.

Length of coastline
750 miles – more if you include every cove.

Highest mountain
Snowdon – at 1,085m, 3,560ft.

Castles
Wales has more castles, for its size, than anywhere else in Europe - there are more than 600, ranging from Edward I's imposing fortresses to modest earthworks and local defences.

Patron saint
St David – celebrated on 1 March.

National emblems
The Welsh Dragon, the leek and the daffodil are seen on flags, official crests, company logos and sports shirts all over Wales.

The Photographers

Aled Hughes
Andrew Davies
Andrew McCartney
Andrew Orchard
Andy Stoyle
Billy Stock
Brian Woods
Chris Colclough
Chris Gallagher
Chris Warren
David Angel
Dave Newbould
David Williams
David Woodfall
Derec Owen
Derek Rees
Duncan Miller
Geraint Wyn Jones
Graham Morley
Harry Williams
Janet and Colin Bord
Jeff Morgan
Jeremy Moore
John Kinsey
Kathy de Witt
Ken Dickinson
Ken Price
Neil Turner
Paul Kay
Pierino Algieri
Ray Wood
Rex Moreton
Rob Stratton
Steve Benbow
Steve Lewis
Steve Peake

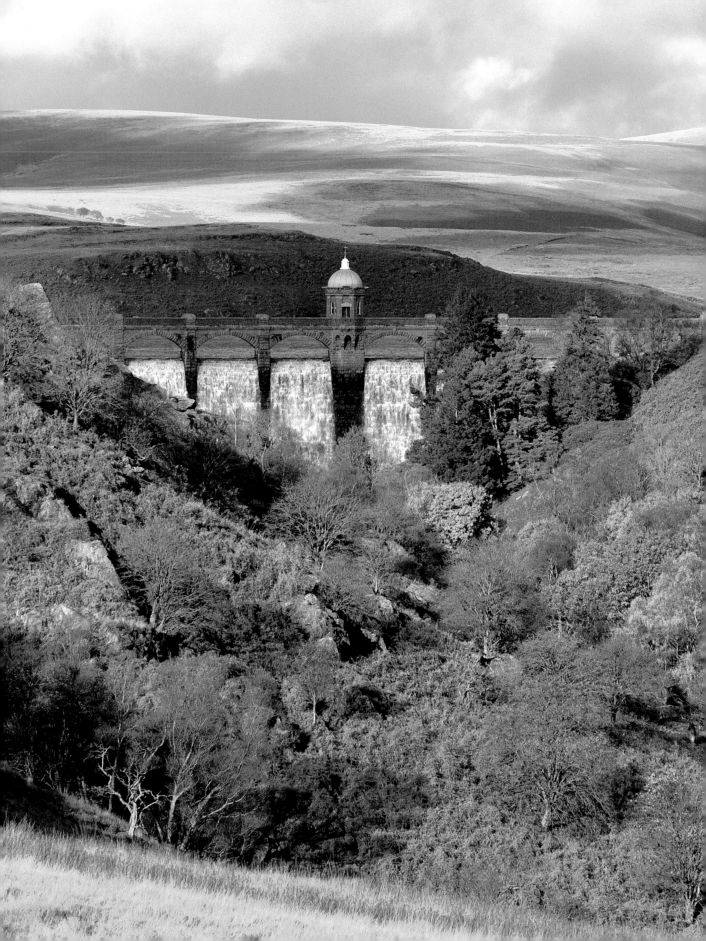